Philip Pearson works as a full-time official for the Transport and General Workers Union in the hotel, catering and contract-cleaning industries. He is a member of two of the wages councils which cover hotels and catering. **Twilight Robbery** is written in an individual capacity.

Philip Pearson

Twilight robbery

Low-paid workers in Britain today

Pluto Press
London and Sydney

First published in 1985 by Pluto Press Limited,
The Works, 105a Torriano Avenue, London NW5 2RX
and Pluto Press Australia Limited, PO Box 199, Leichhardt,
New South Wales 2040, Australia

Copyright © Philip Pearson 1985

Cover designed by Keith Pointing
Set by Grassroots, London NW6
Printed in Great Britain by Guernsey Press, Guernsey C.I.

ISBN 0 86104 647 1

Contents

Preface / 8
Acknowledgements / 11

1. **Survival of the cheapest?** / 12
   Seven million on low wages / 14
   More equal than others? / 16
   Removing the safety net / 19
   The free marketeers / 21
   The unions: adapt and survive / 25

2. **A multitude of sins** / 28
   Rules that divide / 29
   Hard day, low pay / 30
   Working at the Grand / 32
   No room for charity / 34
   Grimmer times in the garment trade / 35
   Set up for the sack / 37
   Immigration controls: iron hand in an iron glove / 38
   The cash con / 40

3. **'The mop'** / 42
   A community organises / 43
   Trouble in store / 47
   Crossing the barriers / 49

4. **Queensland Pleaters** / 52
   An industry in decline / 53
   Rules of the 'sweating' game / 55
   Pressed into dispute / 56
   The strike reassessed / 58

5. **Sunset on Rowton's empire** / 62
   Rooms for the 'deserving poor' / 62
   Working for Rowton / 64
   Agreement made and broken / 65
   Build-up to public acquisition / 68
   Working together / 70

6. **Trade union law** / 72
   Protecting the individual activist / 73
   The 1980 Employment Act / 75
   Second-class workers / 77
   Recognition rights removed / 78
   Cutting through the jungle: new union rights / 82

7. **Wage protection** / 85
   'Fair Wages' abandoned / 86
   The threat to wages councils / 89
   Young workers: the substitution trick / 95
   Breaking with convention / 97

8. **Going through the motions** / 100
   Women: low pay, low priority / 101
   Labour moves / 104
   New partners, old priorities? / 107
   The 1983 general election / 109

9. **Trapped in tradition? Union pay campaigns** / 112
   Wages councils and the unions / 112
   Striking a new bargain / 116
   Negotiator's checklist / 124

10. **Strategy for a fair wage** / 126
    The third course / 127
    Involving the bystanders / 128
    Support for collective bargaining / 129
    'Fair wages' legislation / 133
    End low pay! / 136

   A guide to reading / 138
   List of abbreviations / 142

Preface

One in three of the working population — over seven million people — is low paid, and the number is growing. For these workers, 'twilight robbery' means jobs often on the margins of the economy — in basement kitchens, ill-lit garment factories or in office blocks at dawn. They are denied their due not only through the erosion of already meagre wages but also because of worsening conditions of employment. This robbery by stealth takes place in ways which few people, sometimes even workers themselves, fully appreciate.

There's nothing new about low pay. It's just more important now than at any time since the end of the war because it is central to the Thatcher government's economic policies. Since the 1983 general election it has become at least as significant as unemployment in Tory schemes for the economy.

I hope those who read this book — especially women and men in low paid jobs and those involved in trade union activities — will find it useful in understanding the breadth of the present government's low wages strategy and in anticipating the measures that might follow. Some of the chapters describe struggles to win union recognition and better conditions, particularly on the part of the women and migrant workers, and show how important victories can be won.

This book is also offered as a contribution to the debate on policies for the low paid within the labour movement, in the hope that it will encourage trade union and Labour Party branches to insist that the next round of socialist economic plans do not shunt low pay into a siding. If low pay has become a central economic priority for the government it must then become a central issue for the labour movement, too.

Chapter 1 sets out a vital part of the Thatcher government's monetarist strategy: that wage cuts must take place in order to reduce unemployment. It summarises the facts and figures on low pay, especially among women and black workers, suggesting that the government's low-wage programme is a challenge which the trade unions have yet to take up.

Chapter 2 describes the experiences of individual low-paid workers, particularly women and migrants employed in the service industries.

Chapter 3, 4 and 5 discuss some recent unionisation drives by the low-paid in the clothing, cleaning and hotel industries. How did the workers organise themselves? What can be learnt from the strikes described?

Chapter 6 is about the general attack on workers' rights, which has especially penalised active trade unionists. The government describes employment protection rights as 'rigidities' in the labour market, which must be removed. The chapter also suggests new measures which would assist the low-paid to obtain union recognition.

Chapter 7 examines three key aspects of the government's onslaught on wages: the abolition of the 'Fair Wages' resolution; the threat to scrap the wages councils; and the schemes for young unemployed people, who are being used as little more than cheap labour in an unsuccessful attempt to 'price them back into work'.

Chapter 8 outlines the debate on low pay within the labour movement in recent years. It attempts to explain how it is that the movement's alternative economic strategies have concentrated on economic planning and industrial democracy. Low pay has remained a side issue, in spite of a series of union conference resolutions and campaigns demanding action.

Chapter 9 is about the TUC's two-pronged low-pay campaign, which is intended to concentrate on the defence of wages councils and on the improvement of collective bargaining to assist the low-paid. But both initiatives contain contradictions for the unions which threaten to stall any serious campaigning.

Chapter 10 argues that a positive alternative is urgently needed to the government's low-wages strategy. Labour's alternative programme sees unemployment as the key priority. To appeal to the rapidly growing number of low-paid workers, fresh alternatives are needed — a strategy for a fair wage, for greater equality for women and black workers, and real opportunities for the low-paid to unionise themselves. Such alternatives are developed in this final chapter.

Acknowledgements

In writing this book I have drawn from my experiences as a district officer with the TGWU. To those in this and other unions whose low-pay struggles are described here, many thanks for your assistance; I hope that I have done justice to your efforts. A very warm thank you to Pam Gudgin, Dave Turnbull, Jo Sinclair, Irene Bruegel, Barney Shuster, Maggie Foy, Neil Kearney, members of the Latin American Workers Association, the Migrants Action Group and the Union of Turkish Workers for their advice. Special thanks to Ruth Elliott, Anne Phillips, Roy Green and Dominic Byrne for their comments on early drafts; to Nony Ardill for her detailed work on the final version; to Richard Kuper for his valuable editorial assistance; to those who were interviewed, though I have had to change your names in the text; to Bernie for the mints; and to everyone at Dalston: Jonathon, Francesca and Ros. I owe a great deal to you all.

1. Survival of the cheapest?

In January 1984, Jill's wage was cut. 'Our supervisor came round and told us, "You're going to have to take a drop in pay." There was no letter or anything. Just a cut from £2.12 an hour down to £1.85.'

Jill works as part-time cleaner for Industrial Cleaning Services, at the Royal Artillery Barracks in Greenwich. ICS run the contract at the barracks for the Ministry of Defence, where they employ 39 women cleaners, full- and part-time. Jill said:

> A couple of the full-timers went round with a petition. We all signed it. Some went off to see a solicitor. So the company wrote out a new contract saying £1.95 an hour, but we all handed them back. Then they cancelled a meeting at 8.30 in the morning. Some of us could see what it was — blackmail. You either sign or get out. There would be two weeks' holiday instead of four! If we did not sign, then the company would have no alternative but to stop the contract.
>
> We told them we were going to join a union. 'You know what will happen,' the boss said. 'Unions mean no more tea breaks — you're not entitled to them because you are only part-time. You will be clocking in. It'll all be to rule.' But we drink our tea standing up, anyway, on the job!
>
> I told him that if we join the union and worked a quarter-hour overtime we would get paid for it, and he didn't know what to say. I was so wild when some of them signed that form. We should give them a run for their money.

Jill works a two-and-a-half hour day, five days a week, at the barracks which are within walking distance of her council flat. Although she is still expected to do exactly the same amount of cleaning, the cuts have cost her about £2.12 a week, together with the loss of a fortnight's paid holiday a year. In total, she has lost £159 a year for cleaning the same soldiers' floors.

I would like you to see the building I have to do. It has three storeys with six rooms to a floor. My hours are 7.30 to 10a.m. The soldiers start coming in at 8, so we have to get quite a lot of the cleaning done before they arrive. I have half-an-hour to get the equipment, open the offices, get the rooms ready. But they know I get there at 7.15 to get the work done. I should be paid for at least three-and-a-half hours' work a day, anyway — not two-and-a-half for the actual work I do! The floor is still wet when 50 or 60 soldiers come in with their muddy boots, so it gets filthy again. It's really hard work. To get it done properly, I ought to be starting at half-past six in the morning.

It seems as though they are trying to make the poor poorer. It is frightening what they can do. They can go down to £1 an hour — there are plenty of people looking for jobs. That's the idea, probably.

The government claims that people like Jill 'have priced themselves out of jobs', by demanding wages that are too high. Pay has been held at artificially high levels, so the government would allege, by trade union activities, wage regulations and employment rights. The main aim of present government policy is to force pay down. Laws which once protected trade unionists, wages and jobs have been scrapped.

The wages councils, which provide a floor to wages in many low-paid jobs, are under threat of abolition by the government. In the private sector, these changes mean that firms can reduce labour costs and increase profits. In the public sector, as we shall show, they mean that the government can achieve major savings in public expenditure. 'Privatisation' adds a further twist to the cuts: as services are taken over by private contractors in areas like catering or cleaning, for example — so wages and other working conditions are further eroded. Cuts implemented by contractors make those public-sector workers still employed by the health service or local authorities seem relatively well-off. Only recently, though, they were thought to be among the lowest paid.

The policy of cutting wages is the centrepiece of the government's monetarist economics. One purpose is the old Tory aim: to boost private profits. Another is a familiar Tory theme: to cut public spending. But the third aim — to use wage cuts as a way of solving the unemployment crisis by 'pricing people back into work' — is the creation of the new right-wing leadership of the Conservative Party. The number of low-paid workers is steadily increasing as the wages of many of those who are already low paid, like Jill, are dropping.

The low-wage strategy is a fundamental challenge to trade unions in Britain, for it hits at the heart of the organised labour movement's historic role of defending the wage packet. How the trade unions respond at this crucial time is the main concern of this book. It is apparently recognised in the TUC that government policy is creating greater inequality in wages. Why, then, despite the evidence that the ranks of the low-paid are swelling day by day, has there been no effective counter-campaign against the government? Is it because of the short-sighted belief that the majority of the low-paid are women or young workers? And that, for them, low pay 'doesn't matter so much'? Is it a reflection of the old union belief that men are the breadwinners, and only men need to earn a full 'family wage'? Or is it due to the fact that unemployment is still seen by the unions and the Labour Party as the primary issue?

Seven million on low wages

Most definitions of low pay agree with the minimum wage target set by the TUC: that no worker, male or female, should earn less than two-thirds the average wage of men in manual jobs. Early in 1984, the average wage for men in manual work stood at about £147 per week. Accordingly, the TUC minimum wage target was £98 for a full-time, 40-hour week, or £2.45 per hour. The target is seen by the TUC as a guideline for union negotiators wishing to eliminate low pay. Of course, it is a *moving target* because wages steadily increase, as a result of increases in the cost of living. It is also a minimum *equal* pay target because it applies equally to men and women at work, whether in full- or part-time jobs. The target wage, therefore, implies the lessening of inequality — not only between men and women, but between the lowest- and the better-paid. The Council of Europe has established a 'decency threshold' of earnings to give workers and their dependants a reasonable standard of living. Their formula is that no wage should be less than 68 per cent of average earnings. In Britain, in January 1984, this would have been about £106 per week — or somewhat higher than the TUC's target wage.

The TUC minimum wage is also close to the absolute poverty line for a family of four on supplementary benefits. The level of supplementary benefits is fixed by parliament each year and acts as a safety net. So, for example, a family of two parents and two young children would receive a basic benefit of £66.25 a week in 1984, excluding rent and rates. In its publication *Low Pay and Poverty in the 80s* the Low Pay Unit estimated that for 1983—4 such a family would need gross earnings of £105.45 a week to give a net weekly wage equal to their supplementary benefit. In the same report it was calculated that, in 1983, over seven million workers earned less than £100 a week gross, or £2.50 an hour. This total includes four million full-time and over three million part-time workers. The estimates exclude workers' earnings from overtime. Men in manual jobs rely on overtime more than other workers to boost their pay. If overtime is excluded from our calculations, fair comparisons can be made between the number of full- and part-timers earning low *basic* wages (see Table 1).

Nearly two-thirds of full-timers and nearly 90 per cent of part-timers on low pay are women. Altogether, about one-third of the entire working population is low paid. As the Low Pay Unit concluded, low pay is not a fringe issue, 'it permeates our economy and society'.

Table 1 How many low-paid?

	Women	Men	Total
Full-time workers – under £100 a week	2.4 million	1.6 million	4 million
Part-time workers – under £2.50 an hour	2.7 million	0.4 million	3.1 million
All workers	5.1 million	2.0 million	7.1 million

Source: Low Pay Unit, 1983.

More equal than others?

Unequal pay for women persists, despite the 1970 Equal Pay Act. Women with family commitments can usually take less advantage of overtime and bonus schemes than men, so average earnings for women are about 65p for every £1 earned by men. The notion that men are the 'breadwinners' runs deep in British society, and lies at the root of the problem of low wages among women. When it is pointed out that many of the low-paid are women or young people, many trade unionists automatically see it as less of a problem. Why should a teenager earn the adult rate? Can't a woman rely on her husband's or children's earnings? Shouldn't a man be able to earn enough to support his family?

The idea of a man needing a 'family wage' developed in the nineteenth century. Legislation and public policy gradually restricted the employment of children and then women from many areas of work. As legislation and trade union pressure took effect, skilled male workers demanded a wage to keep the whole family as compensation for these changes. In the twentieth century, this same argument has been exploited by employers and union negotiators – effectively dividing working people by setting a separate, higher rate for men's work. For women who have to work, the myth of the family wage makes for considerable hardship. Today, only about one household in 20 conforms to the stereotype of working man, wife at home not in paid work, two young children. Nearly one million households are headed by a single parent, the majority of whom are women, dependent on women's wages or getting by on social security benefits. In nearly 400,000 wage-earning households, the woman is the sole earner due to her husband's unemployment. Overall, in about one-quarter of households, women provide the main or only means of financial support.

Furthermore, earnings of black workers are less than those of white workers doing similar jobs. In 1984, Colin Brown produced the results of a major national survey conducted in 1982 of living and working conditions of Asian, West Indian and white people in Britain. His report, *Black and White Britain*, showed that for black men there is a 'pattern of inequality' in earnings for jobs at all levels. Average earnings of white males in the survey were about £136 in 1982, or some £20 higher than the average for black men, despite the fact that blacks were more likely to work shifts or unsocial hours. The wages of unskilled black women were generally not significantly less than those of unskilled white women — both groups earning around £72 to £76 per week. Colin Brown does not miss the irony of the situation: 'The enormous disparity between men and women in this respect left little scope for racial disadvantage to have a further effect' on black women's earnings.

The low-pay league

Table 2 charts the 'bottom ten' jobs for men and women, in terms of average hourly earnings. Almost every industry has at least some employees working for low wages. The contradictions between pay and workplace can be extreme: night cleaners in luxuriously appointed city-centre offices are among the lowest paid in Britain; receptionists in hotels are expected to present an efficient, welcoming, even glamorous face to the public, but their wages may well be a pittance.

The main concentrations of low-waged work are in service industries — shops, hotels and catering, distribution, cleaning, hospital portering. The Low Pay Unit estimated that more than half of all full-time, low-paid workers are employed in the service

Table 2 Low-pay league, 1983

Full-time workers	Average hourly earnings (£s)*	Average gross weekly earnings (£s)*	Average weekly hours of work**	% of workers earning under £100 (gross) a week**
Women				
Hairdressers	1.58	60.50	38½	94
Waitresses	1.88	72.50	38½	87
Bar staff	1.89	77.20	41	83
Shop assistants	1.91	73.40	38	94
Check-out operators	1.91	74.90	39	92
Sewing machinists	1.98	77.60	39	86
Kitchen hands	2.00	75.70	37½	86
Counter hands	2.06	80.30	38½	84
Cleaners	2.09	81.80	39	81
Receptionists	2.14	80.10	37½	82
Average: all manual jobs	2.22	87.90	39	73
Men				
General farm workers	2.19	103.40	46	53
Bar staff	2.24	105.70	47	51
Farm-machinery drivers	2.28	111.60	46½	44
Agricultural stock men	2.38	122.30	49	24
Hospital porters	2.44	113.10	45	34
Caretakers	2.47	109.80	44	46
Road-sweepers	2.48	109.20	43	43
Butchers, meat-cutters	2.52	111.30	43½	46
Cleaners	2.57	118.70	44½	35
Gardeners, groundsmen	2.57	106.60	41	46
Average: all manual jobs	3.19	143.60	44	16

* Excluding overtime.
** Including overtime.

Source: *New Earnings Survey*, 1983.

sector. The 1983 *New Earnings Survey* also reveals that low-paid, part-time jobs, with an hourly rate of less than £2.50, are even more ghettoised in the service industries. High proportions of workers in these jobs are women and from the ethnic minority communities. Even in the same low-paid jobs — such as bar work or cleaning — women's hourly rates of pay are less than men's. On average, women's full-time hourly rates are about 74 per cent of men's. Lower hourly pay and less overtime working mean that, compared with men, more full-time women wage-earners earn under £100 a week. Overall, the weekly earnings of women in manual jobs were about £88 in 1983; for men, the sum was around £144.

Removing the safety net

Government ministers question the future of wages councils, arguing that they keep pay at artificially high levels. However, these bodies play an important part in protecting the low-paid from wage undercutting. Trade unions have had long-standing reservations about wages councils, which were once considered to lessen the necessity for the low-paid to join a union and negotiate better pay and conditions (see chapter 9).

The wages council machinery has been in force since 1909, when the Trade Boards Act allowed for the fixing of minimum rates in poorly unionised trades where pay was 'exceptionally low as compared with other employments'. The 1945 Wages Council Act set the councils up in their present form. Today, there are 27 wages councils (Table 3), covering some 2,734,800 workers. The minimum rates of pay which they set are enforced by the wages inspectorate, though government cuts in the staff of the inspectorate have reduced its effectiveness. The majority of the minimum rates lie between £60 and £68 a week for a full-time job. The councils are independent bodies, each made up of representatives from trade unions' and employers' organisations, and three independent members. The latter conciliate between the two sides when wages, holiday entitlement and a limited range of other working conditions are revised each year.

Industries covered by wages councils are poorly unionised,

ranging from almost nil union membership in hairdressing, through to about 10 per cent in catering and around 40 per cent in the clothing industry. Overall, perhaps a quarter of the workers in the remaining wages councils are union members, though less are covered by a union recognition agreement. About three-quarters of workers covered by the councils are women. In addition to these bodies, there are national agricultural wages boards which set minimum rates for a further 275,000 farmworkers. As Chris Pond has shown in his contribution to *Industrial Relations in Britain*, wages councils and boards protect about one-fifth of the country's full-time workers and around one-third of adult low-paid workers.

Table 3 Wages council industries

Industry	No. workers	No. wages councils
Hotel and catering	1,180,400	3
Retail trades	1,037,300	3
Clothing	278,400	8
Laundries	33,700	1
Hairdressing	135,600	1
Toy manufacture	18,900	1
Waste reclamation	19,300	1
Miscellaneous trades	31,200	9
Total	2,734,800	27

Source: Department of Employment.

The double standards in pay which afflict women in other industries are also found in the wages-council sector, where average hourly rates for women in manual jobs are around three-quarters of those for men, and only two-thirds of the male rate in non-manual positions. In 1983, average hourly earnings for female manual workers in this sector were just £1.89 an hour compared with £2.42 an hour for men. Indeed, given the substantial problem of employers paying below even these minimal rates, it would appear that women must suffer particularly from illegal underpayment. Yet, as we suggest in chapter 9, because of the low level of union organisation the abolition of the councils is likely to lead to a wage collapse in these industries.

Left out in the cold
Neither the Department of Employment (the government department with responsibility for wages councils and the inspectorate) nor the TUC has made an estimate of the number of low-paid workers who are already outside the scope of a wages council and a union recognition agreement. It would be a massive task to undertake for the whole of industry, for low pay is widespread. Yet there are gaping holes in the wages council safety net. Perhaps 500,000 workers ought, logically, to be included within the ambit of a wages council because of the similar nature of the work they do, their low earnings and low level of union affiliation. Yet they are, as Table 4 shows, left out in the cold.

The free marketeers

John Selwyn Gummer, then minister for employment, gave the government's views on low pay in a House of Commons debate on the issue in February 1984: 'the number of people who have a job will directly depend on the levels of pay received by those in work.'

His government's campaign to reduce wages has been fought on three fronts: unemployment, the abolition of wage and employment protection and the 'privatisation' of public services. Together, these measures are extremely effective. High unemployment creates tension between those with a job and those without. Today, employers can declare with real force, 'If you don't like the job, then I can soon find someone else who will do it.' Recently, 600 people applied for 17 trainee managers' jobs with a West London hotel group. Firms can pick and choose, offering jobs at lower rates as workers leave, or replacing them with young workers on one of the government schemes. They need be less concerned now about workers' rights, for the government believes that firms should be able to buy labour in the same way that people purchase soap flakes or newspapers, and has acted to turn this belief into reality.

Table 4 No wages council protection

Wages council industry	Jobs not covered
Hotel and catering	Industrial staff canteens; contract catering; unlicensed hotels and hostels; boarding houses
Retail trades	Florists; jewellers; chemists; photocopy shops; butchers; shops selling bathroom goods; opticians; pet shops; record shops; motor accessory shops; estate agents; travel agents
Clothing	Leather workers; sub-contracted work such as pleating, making clothing extras (knitwear, gloves, tights, etc.); clerical, cleaning staff
Laundries	Launderette attendants if they do not do washing; workers employed by dry cleaners to do alterations
Hairdressing	Beauty therapists
Other jobs	Petrol pump attendants; contract cleaning; various contract work such as delivery work; homeworkers not covered by a wages council; security services; telephone sales; warehousing; office services such as envelope addressing; temporary working such as secretarial or clerical

Chapter 6 describes how the government has repealed measures to assist the process of trade unionisation and weakened safeguards for active trade unionists against unfair dismissal. With the erosion of other basic rights at work, there is now a growing body of workers in smaller establishments who have very little protection against arbitrary management decisions. Various kinds of wage regulation have been abolished. In its first parliament, the government scrapped Schedule 11 of the 1975 Employment Protection Act. This Act had helped trade unions ensure that employers paid nationally agreed minimum rates, and to establish the fair rate for a job should an employer try to undercut agreed working conditions. In September 1983, the government scrapped the long-standing 'Fair Wages' resolution of parliament, which had prevented government departments from hiving off work to outside contractors unless they offered fair minimum wages and conditions.

Jill had not been aware that her wages were protected by the 'Fair Wages' resolution. Her employer was obliged to offer a rate of pay and other conditions, such as holidays, which were at least comparable with those of workers employed by a local authority for similar work. In December 1982 Norman Tebbit, when employment secretary, announced that the government was not going to renew the resolution — though the decision to put this into effect was delayed until after the June 1983 general election. In August 1983 the Ministry of Defence wrote to all its cleaning contractors at barracks and office blocks throughout the country, instructing them to revise their contracts as they were no longer obliged to pay minimum wages and holidays: 'The contractor will be entirely responsible for setting the pay and conditions of staff.' Thus, the market would dictate wages in the absence of effective union negotiating or rights at work.

Because of high unemployment, and encouraged by the government, firms have been able to cut wages. Similar pressures have been applied to health service administrators, who have been instructed 'not to specify rates of pay or conditions of service for contractors' staff' when putting work to private tender (Circular DA8340). This incitement to health authorities to ignore national joint wage agreements has met with forceful union opposition. To date, only some 2.1 per cent of health service expenditure on ancillary services such as catering goes to outside contractors. This is due mainly to trade union campaigns against cuts in working conditions, and to the fact that health service administrators have been unimpressed by the quality of service provided by contractors.

Privatisation of services opens the door to the so-called 'free market' for labour, which becomes the sole arbiter of wages and conditions. But the free market knows no standards except profitability. There appears to be virtually no limit to how far the market can drag down the working conditions of employees who are on contract to the public sector. For example, in March 1984, 92 cleaners at Barking Hospital, East London, were sacked by their employers, Crothalls Ltd. The cleaners had gone on strike after Redbridge Health Authority had accepted a new Crothalls contract offering to cut wages by an average of 35 per cent, abolish sick pay and cut holidays by a quarter. Many Conservative-controlled local education authorities are following the lead of central government and contracting-out their school meals and cleaning services. Savings are being achieved — but once again at the price of poorer working conditions, and lower standards for the children.

Other new 'freedoms' are appearing in the labour market. In 1983, the Commission for Racial Equality published a code of practice for the elimination of racial discrimination and the promotion of equal employment opportunities. But Norman Tebbit, as employment secretary, insisted that firms with less than 200 workers should be exempt from the code.

'Creeping underdevelopment' is how Paul Harrison described the effect of these policies in his book *Inside the Inner City*. He believes that the country is slipping back into an economy of coolie labour, by the creation of a 'Third World economy in our midst' in the inner-city areas and the depressed regions. Industries like the garment trade have been devastated by cheap imports from such Third World nations as the Philippines and Bangladesh. In response, working conditions in the industry in Britain are beginning to mirror those abroad (see the case study in Chapter 4). Earnings of manual workers have been hardest hit by government policies. According to *Low Wages and Poverty in the 80s*, one in ten men in manual jobs earned low wages in 1979; by 1983 this proportion has increased to one in every six. Amongst women in manual jobs, two-thirds were low paid in

1979; in 1983 the proportion had increased to four out of five.

The unions: adapt and survive

Alongside the creation of a growing low-wage sector, changes are taking place within the British economy with further implications for trade unions. Traditional areas of well-unionised, predominantly male employment in manufacturing industries are on the decline. Their place is being taken by service industries which employ mainly women or young workers, offering opportunities for part-time work where the level of trade union membership is much lower. The workplaces are typically smaller than the large factories of the 1960s and 1970s, whose size made union organisation economic. Instead, unions now organise penny packets of workers, often in the face of an anti-union management. The low-wage service sector is expanding as yet unchallenged in any serious way by trade union collective bargaining.

In 1983, economists at the University of Warwick estimated that service industries would expand by some 200,000 jobs between 1983 and 1987. Almost all the net gain would be in employment for women, especially in part-time work. In the economy as a whole, total employment was expected to decline slightly, especially in manufacturing, due to such factors as the low level of investment and competition from imports. Assessments such as these contradict the central claim made by the government: that if wages are forced down, workers will 'price themselves back into work'. Almost all economic forecasts predict a continuously high level of unemployment under existing policies. The government's claim is also countered by evidence from the Young Workers Scheme (see chapter 7), which indicates that, despite low wages, these schemes do not create employment chances for the young. The only increase they produce is in profit levels of firms who can switch to employing labour at cheaper rates. The low-wage strategy discourages company investment: why should firms invest to increase their efficiency and productivity when cheap labour is available? Yet this disincentive to invest puts an even greater premium on keeping the wage bill down. Furthermore, cuts in health and education services through contracting-out are also leading to a fall in the quality of the services bought, with people working harder than the reasonable limit and private firms cutting all sorts of corners to meet profit targets.

In summary, it would appear that the government's strategy is creating three sectors of labour: the unemployed; low-paid workers in service industries and in low-technology industries, like clothing; and higher-paid workers, probably using higher technology, in some areas of manufacturing and of white-collar work (banking, insurance, finance, information industries, for example). These broad changes in the economy, continually stimulated by the monetarist assault on wages, are a major challenge to the unions.

Estimates suggest that between 1979 and 1983, total union membership in Britain fell by nearly three million. In the years of rapid growth in their membership during the 1970s, unions could afford the luxury of concentrating their activities on the larger workplaces — which were more economic to service and provided greater industrial influence. Those days have slipped by as manufacturing firms cut back their labour or close down and as the service sector expands. Medium and small establishments in the service industries are the main recruiting ground of the future. These places, especially those in the service sector, employ more women, migrant workers, part-timers and casuals than the unions have been used to enlisting in the past. Recruitment methods will have to be adapted to meet the new situation.

Unionisation drives are likely to be more labour intensive, largely because of the greater number of places to be visited. In a hostile industrial and political climate, the failure rate of union campaigns is higher. Trade unions may need to re-examine their organisational strategies, perhaps placing greater emphasis on education for new, inexperienced members, revising courses to include less familiar topics — women's rights, racial discrimination, equal pay, recruitment methods. Traditional ways of servicing smaller workplaces may prove to be uneconomic for the unions, so that servicing strategies may demand fundamental administrative changes, as well. Some of these recruitment and organisational questions are discussed in the next chapters of this book. But the labour movement as a whole urgently needs a counter-strategy to match the government's monetarist programme of low wages and high unemployment. An alternative economic strategy which argues for equality, fair wages and economic growth should be clearly recognisable to the growing numbers of people without work or getting by on low wages. Finding this new strategy is the challenge which seven million low-paid workers now present to the unions.

2. A multitude of sins

Low-paid jobs involve a multitude of sins. Quite apart from low wages there are other disadvantages. Workers are more likely to need overtime earnings to make up for low basic rates, or to take two jobs — a chambermaid may work part-time as a supermarket check-out operator, a chef may have an evening cleaning job. Both occupations will be low-paid; neither may offer much in the way of paid holidays or a company sickness scheme.

Many employers fix the wages of part-time jobs just below the limit for national insurance contributions, set by the government at £34 a week in 1984. The Low Pay Unit suggested that nearly 2.25 million part-timers had earnings that fell just short of this figure in 1984. As soon as a worker's earnings exceed this limit, perhaps with some overtime or a pay rise, national insurance contributions have to be paid on the whole wage packet, so national insurance acts as a kind of 'supertax' for the lowest-paid. The low-paid find all too often that these contributions are not passed on the the DHSS, so that when they go to claim unemployment or maternity benefit or retirement pension, the claim may be disallowed.

A further feature of low-paid work is that health and safety standards are often inadequate, especially if there is no trade union safety representative. Equally, grievance and disciplinary procedures may be a weak defence against arbitrary management decisions — again, especially in smaller, unorganised workplaces. In turn, having a low-paid job is one of the disadvantages of being black, a woman, or both. Chapter 1 showed that women and black workers earn less than white males in equivalent work. Many migrant and immigrant workers initially came to Britain to work, taking jobs which were so poorly paid that they could not be filled at the time by indigenous labour. For example, around 45 per cent of London's hotel and catering workers are from abroad. Overseas workers have found it extremely difficult to break out of the low-wage sector — more so now that unemployment is high.

Rules that divide

It is useful to draw a distinction between migrant and immigrant workers. The great majority of *migrant* workers are from countries outside the Commonwealth (such as the Philippines, Spain, Turkey, Portugal and Latin America) and entered the UK on a work permit. The majority of Commonwealth *immigrants*, on the other hand, either came to Britain before immigration controls were imposed, or, from 1962, entered under the employment voucher scheme. The 1971 Immigration Act abolished vouchers and brought all overseas workers under a single work permit system. During the 1960s, the number of work permits increased and eventually overtook the number of vouchers issued to Commonwealth immigrants. The permit system allowed firms to recruit a worker from overseas if a specific vacancy could not be filled by local labour, and many firms took this opportunity to recruit migrants to jobs whose poor wages and conditions were unattractive to local workers. At the time of the 1971 Immigration Act, the work permit system was tightened up, making it far more difficult for employers to recruit for semi- and unskilled posts. Exceptions were made due to pressure from employers in certain industries, so special quotas were allowed for hotels and catering and for domestic work in hospitals and private homes. Rising unemployment and trade union pressures led to these two quotas being cut back; by 1980, no permits were issued other than for a limited number of skilled workers. By this time, however, around 250,000 migrant workers and their families had come to work in the UK and had settled here.

For employers, one of the attractions of the work permit scheme is that a permit is issued to them rather than to the worker.

The employee's permission to remain in Britain has to be renewed each year, and any change in job needs Department of Employment approval. Only after four years on a permit can the worker apply to the Home Office to become 'free in the country' and then take up any kind of employment. Though the unions intensely disliked this 'fettered labour' system, the Labour government of 1974-9 failed to take the opportunity to improve it.

The majority of migrant workers have been in the UK for over four years and are now free of restrictions on their employment. Yet a substantial number of the rest have considerable difficulties with the immigration authorities and may be working without authorisation in several different ways: their employer may have deceived them into thinking that a permit has been obtained when it has not; many refugees, students and visitors are not permitted to work in Britain but nevertheless do so; they may overstay the period thay were given to remain in the country and continue in employment as 'illegal' workers.

Migrant and immigrant workers frequently remain in the service industries which have a constant demand for cheap labour. Their lack of mobility is encouraged by discrimination in the labour market by employers, though immigration restrictions and language and cultural barriers also play a part. In the rest of this chapter the exploitation of individual low-paid workers is examined in typical low-wage industries: clothing, hotels, restaurants and hostels.

Hard day, low pay

Gary works as a linen porter in a 400-bedroom hotel in West London. 'People look at my wage packet and they see £103, and they say, "That's not bad." I tell them it's for two weeks, after tax. My rent is £31 a week. I must leave and find another job.'

'But stay here and help build the union,' I suggested to him. 'The next job will only be low paid, or pay you a little more.'

'I know, that's the choice,' he replied.

Gary came from Nigeria to work in Britain 14 years ago. He collects up the soiled white sheets, towels and pillowcases that the chambermaids leave in the corridors once the beds have been stripped and the bathrooms cleaned. One sheet is laid out flat and the rest of the linen heaped on top. The four corners of the sheet are brought over and tied together like a giant handkerchief. The bag is humped over a shoulder to the lift. It goes down to the basement where it is stacked in the corridors. Then it is humped out to the laundry van. It's hard, repetitive work.

Tamisa works as a chambermaid in the same hotel.

> We work up on the seventh floor. Today the sweat was pouring off, it's hot up there, the heat goes up in this building. But if we open the windows the dust comes in. The housekeeper comes round to check the rooms so they would need dusting again. It is a bit better in the winter, but what do we get? Our basic pay plus overtime is about £96 every two weeks after tax. To live today you need £100 a week. There's your rent and bills to pay, the gas and electricity. It's hard. The money is very small. Anything extra will help, such as if we can clean extra rooms when the hotel is busy. We get £1.25 for an extra room.

This extra room bonus is taxed; it is worth about 80p cash. In Tamisa's hotel the price of rooms in the winter of 1983 was £30 per night for a single or £41 per night for a twin-bedded room. Each room has a private bathroom; the price includes VAT and a continental breakfast. One manager said, 'The rooms are easier to do now, they have a better design and a simpler layout.' But the company had, like many others in the industry, done away with a room valet service, replacing it with do-it-yourself facilities for making tea and coffee in the room. So the crockery has to be washed, the service area cleaned, the kettle emptied, wiped, replaced, the lead coiled around it, the plug switched off; then there's the provision of fresh milk cartons, coffee, tea and sugar bags. This is all additional work for the room-maid.

Chambermaids may earn roughly the same as the predominantly male linen porters, because both are entitled to the same legal minimum hourly rate of pay set by the wages council for licensed hotels (about £1.68 an hour in 1984). This may seem like equal pay, but it is also equal poverty.

The chambermaid goes to do the next room in the hotel, which the guest has just left. Today, she switches on the TV and works to the morning film. It helps relieve the monotony of her job. Every surface must be dusted, the bed lifted and hoovered beneath. If there are three or four beds in the room — perhaps a double and two singles — each one has to be stripped and remade. As well as introducing tea-bars into the rooms, the company is increasing the number of beds in order to raise the income from each letting.

And then she must clean the toilet and bathroom, lean over and sprinkle bleach powder in the basin, lean over and clean the bath, inhaling fumes. The chambermaid may regret not having put on rubber gloves today, but it is inconvenient to keep taking them off when you don't need them. Dermatitis is a typical, though minor, industrial disease among chambermaids. Instances of hotel companies not providing gloves at all are common.

Working at the Grand

Lisa McHugh works as head housekeeper at the Grand Hotel, central London. She is in charge of nine chambermaids and other staff. Having been active in the union in previous jobs, she encouraged her department to join a union. But the company would not recognise it, so she took up some staff grievances anyway.

> We have asked for better wages because we still only get £68. They are doing heavy work, cleaning at least 13 rooms a day. I tried to get them extra money for extra rooms. Well, at last we were offered something: 50p, irrespective of what size the room is, single, double, treble — it's a flat rate. We were given this on 13 August. Before that, they didn't get paid at all. The rooms cost £16 a single, £27 for a twin with bathroom. I went and saw the acting manager and said we want to get paid because the lasses will not do the rooms.

Despite the low pay, high standards are expected. Small bonuses are given for extra work, which is cheaper than paying overtime rates. The 90,500 chambermaids in hotels in Britain, full- and part-time, work hard for little reward. One traditionally undervalued women's occupation, that of head housekeeper in a hotel, is discussed in more detail in chapter 9. The rate for this job, despite its additional skills and responsibility, may be only £5 or £10 more than that of a chambermaid.

Lisa objected to the poor quality of the equipment available to her staff.

> We've old hoovers and we've no trolleys for the maids. There is no service lift or linen chute so they have to hump the linen on their backs from the sixth floor down. They're like wee pack-horses going about.
>
> They're wanting efficiency to help improve the service, but they won't help us to do so. We housekeepers don't get our uniforms, but they want you to look smart on the floors. I have just paid £40 for this uniform.

Her assistant, Anna, said that she paid £10 for a skirt and £14 for her two blouses.

> That is £24, of my money! In other jobs we've had a spare. We used to get them dry cleaned free of charge through the company, but not here. I came out with £46.78 net last week. I live in the staff accommodation next door. If I was living out, my gross would be £72.25 a week. I couldn't live on it. That's why I chose to live in. Here we start at 7.30 in the morning. It's supposed to be a 40-hour week.
>
> Mrs McHugh and myself have been running the department though there should be three senior staff. They couldn't get anyone else on these wages! We said we could do it between us and get a pay rise, but they refused. We have saved the company £70 a week. If one of us is off, all we have been given is some overtime. We have co-operated together, this is how it has worked. We are the ones who have seen how it can be done without the third worker.

Management had also cut back on staff overtime during the winter season, so cleaning standards in the hotel had suffered.

Other savings had been made: Lisa described the staff food as 'diabolical. It's sausages, beans and chips today, a one-course, one-choice meal, or eat a sandwich. We have not had soup for ages. They even put a note by the milk machine saying staff are not allowed to drink the milk.' Yet there is a legal stipulation in the wages council regulations for licensed hotels such as this that staff food should be 'of good and sufficient quality and quantity'. Employers are allowed to deduct up to £4.80 a week from wages to cover the cost of meals for staff on duty. Sometimes it is hard to remember that the workers are employed in the *catering* industry.

Anna said:

> I collect the union money each week here. I say, 'Right, girls, Christmas club,' because there is usually a manager hanging around on pay day. All those in our department are in. They asked me what happens after Christmas. I said that we will have an Easter club. They feel protected by the union, think it's a good thing, and I have always been in.

Yet the company had, so far, refused to recognise their trade union.

No room for charity

Some of the lowest-paid jobs in Britain are to be found in the hostels for single men and women, run privately or by charitable trusts. Force of circumstance took William Thomas to one of Rowton's men's hostels, Tower House in East London, 11 years ago. It was the only job offering staff accommodation. He said:

> I am not able to cook. I have been brought up practically by the LCC, as it was years ago, in homes. I have spinal meningitis, that is why I am small. I am supposed to be on a diet. I did not get it here at first. When I asked the manager he sent me to see the director, who said I should get it arranged. But I never had it properly sorted out.

William had just failed a medical. He was found to have high blood pressure and to be diabetic. The hostel had just been sold to the Greater London Council and all existing staff had been offered employment — provided they passed the council's medical. Having failed, William would be made redundant. In his last year at the hostel he earned about £26 for a 48-hour week. He would now be rehoused in another nearby hostel — unemployed, though better housed. Ill-health had always restricted his opportunities in the employment 'market'. Now, it would deprive him of a council job with better pay and conditions than he had ever known.

Grimmer times in the garment trade

Maggie Foy, a former official with the National Union of Tailors and Garment Workers, commented that low wages exist throughout the clothing and garment industry. She attributes this to the fact that

> the clothing worker generally is highly skilled, but those skills have never been recognised as such. The workforce do not see themselves as skilled. It's mainly a women's industry and, unfortunately, the women have kept a low profile. In the heyday, the profits were not ploughed back. The majority of employers in London as late as 1979 were using antiquated machinery, producing expensive garments by skilled handsewing, and the wages are grim.

Christina, a Greek Cypriot, has been in England for 25 years, working in the clothing industry for 20 of them. She says:

> Now I have to work more hard than ever. My husband has heart trouble and has not worked for three years. He is getting sickness benefit, but it is not enough for a family of six, especially now my son is at college. So the sickness benefit is nothing. I have to work, I am working without my stamps.
> My job is flat machinist in a factory. Eight years ago I was doing dresses at home for 15 shillings each. Now I am working in a factory and using a machine on piecework. I get 50p for a dress which is harder to make than eight

years ago. Wages come to £80 a week, but to get this the
boss comes round three or four times a day, and if he
thinks you are not doing enough he complains. I was working very hard, doing 40 dresses an hour. You have to do
the whole sleeve from the neck down, plus the sides and
the waist. To do 40 dresses an hour, imagine how the
machine has to work! One hour has got 60 minutes, so that
is even less than two minutes each, and for this I can show
you the boss is not happy. He wants more.

My friends say, 'Forget the time as it used to be.' These
days it doesn't matter how much you push yourself.
Chinese or Turkish or Indian ladies are working at home
now, so all the work from the factory is going to these
people. There are many alterations needed in the work
when it comes in to the factory, but they don't stop them.
They are working cheap.

Her eyes are dark-rimmed. She talks slowly, deliberately, with
a calm direct manner. Her description needs no elaboration.

I know a lady who used to get £150 a week doing dresses
eight hours a day. Now she can't get any real work. They
drop the price of a dress. They pay, for example, 75p each.
But there are some dresses with double the work in them
for the same price.

If I put my stamps on and pay tax, it is good for later on
— I can get a pension. But if I put my stamps on,
straightaway they are not going to give anything to my
husband. I get £80, it will not be enough. What can I do?
Am I right? If you are doing piecework you are always in a
worry. If you get a difficult dress you earn much less in
some weeks. I am a fast worker, but I decided to get paid
by the hour. Believe me, I work very hard, I kill myself
each day. At the factory people have actually fainted. They
have a very short lunch break, work Saturday and Sunday.

Our factory makes over 3,000 dresses a week. But there
are only eight of us. We have to tidy up and sweep up on a
Friday, and if it is half-past five and we have not finished,
he won't pay us. If we are busy and he wants us in on

Saturday, he says, 'If you are not coming Saturday, you are not coming Monday.'

If all the women from Cyprus and the Chinese girls and the women from Turkey get together and say we won't do the dresses for this much, the price we get will go up.

Many small entrepreneurs who set up in the clothing industry are from the same community as their employees — Turkish or Greek Cypriot, for example. The capital invested may be low, the machines will probably be rented, and the premises may even be a house and certain to lack protection against the risk of fire from, say, over-loaded power points. Community ties do not prevent exploitation; indeed, such small firms may offer the only local work for women from the same community with family commitments.

Set up for the sack

Sue worked at a restaurant in the City of London as a barmaid. After six months' service, she was asked during a slack period in the summer to work in the kitchen for a fortnight, which she agreed to do. At the end of this period, Sue was told by the manager to go to another branch which was short of staff and needed help in the kitchen preparing salads. This time, Sue objected, pointing out that there was nothing in her contract to indicate that she had to accept a transfer.

The manager then produced the job application form to show a section which stated that staff must be willing to work anywhere in London or the South-East of England. The manager claimed that it gave him the right to send her anywhere in the region. She went under protest to the other branch. On arrival, she was instructed to work on the grill rather than prepare salads. She refused, believing that she was not qualified to do the job she was sent to do, was sent back to her branch and formally suspended. She turned to her staff representative for advice: though he was a union member, like herself, the company did not recognise a union, and instead had a system of staff representatives to assist in grievance and disciplinary matters. When the staff representative complained that the suspension was unfair, the manager walked out of the office. The following morning, Sue was advised that management was prepared to forget the incident if she would give an assurance that, in future, she would comply with any directive that management might give. Sue replied that if this would include being transferred to other branches, she could not agree. She was then sacked.

The staff representative helped her to arrange an appeal, at which it was pointed out that Sue had been dismissed without first being given a verbal or written warning; in any case, the incident itself did not involve gross misconduct and did not warrant instant dismissal. She was reinstated with a formal verbal warning and then left for a fortnight's holiday. When she returned, Sue found a letter from the manager confirming the verbal warning. On the second day back, she was called in to see the assistant manager, who accused her of having a 'lackadaisical and uncooperative attitude', of not paying attention that day during a staff-training period and of being rude to a customer. She was given a first written warning. The staff representative arranged an immediate appeal to the general manager, arguing that Sue was hardly back from holiday, that the matters themselves did not justify a written warning, that the assistant manager had waited until the general manager had gone out before issuing the warning, though he should have been present. But the general manager refused to withdraw the warning: although Sue had 'nice legs' her attitude was wrong. After two hours she walked out of the office telling them to 'stuff their job'. Later, when she calmed down, she handed in her notice.

The staff representative summed up the sacking by arguing that management had had to back down the first time because they hadn't followed their procedure correctly, so 'the second time they got to her by "going through the procedure". It was obviously a set-up by both of them. Their attitude towards her was appalling.'

Immigration controls: iron hand in an iron glove

Maria is a Portuguese shop steward in a hotel in Euston. In

November 1983, police and immigration service officials visited her hotel. She said:

> Three CID officers and a woman came to the hotel. They walked in, early in the morning and took three people to the police station. They said there was a report or a letter informing them that there were illegal people in the hotel. They took a Moroccan, a French boy and a Spanish woman; she had a visa but no permission to work. Spain is not in the Common Market yet.

It is most unlikely that the police would have had prior informaation on the three so-called illegal workers from such different backgrounds and nationalities. It is more likely that they visited the hotel on the basis of a single piece of information, cast their net and took away three people. A number of staff walked out of the hotel that day as soon as the police had left, and did not return for some days.

These raids increase the insecurity of migrant and immigrant workers. Their effect spreads far beyond those actually arrested. Other staff who are still on work permits, people who may have applied for, but not yet been granted, British citizenship, or those who are questioned because of the colour of their skin − all will be intimidated by these 'fishing expeditions' by the police.

In a hotel near Maria's, one of the bar staff, a Thailander, is facing deportation. He came to Britain in 1975 to study English, and took a part-time job to supplement his small income. At the end of this course he decided to extend his studies. He was well liked by the employer, who offered him a permanent job − but was unable to obtain a work permit. Indeed, it is most unlikely that a permit would have been granted, even under the old 'hotel and catering' quota, because the Home Office would be reluctant to agree to a change in his immigration status from that of an overstaying student to a fully authorised work permit holder.

Unfortunately for him, in one sense, he then met and fell in love with a Filipina working in Britain. She was employed on a valid work permit. They were married in London and now have a two-year-old child. Somehow, the Home Office found out about him. He was visited by the police at work, taken away and imprisoned. His formal appeals against deportation as an alleged 'overstayer' have failed, although he was soon released from prison. His wife has worked in Britain for over four years, is now 'free in the country', and has applied for British citizenship. The deportation threatens to break up their family, or to land them on foreign soil, although Britain is their true 'home' country. Their trade union has lodged an appeal with the home secretary, arguing for the deportation order to be lifted on compassionate grounds. The harsh application of immigration controls is an issue which many migrants want their unions to oppose.

The cash con

Mehmet Polat worked as a tailor's presser for Inan Fashions of Newington Green, North London. One day, Mehmet decided to visit the local law centre, believing that his employer was not paying tax or national insurance deductions to the relevant authorities. As soon as the employer was contacted, however, Mehmet was sacked; his wife, Zeynep, who worked at the same factory, was dismissed at the same time. Their union, the National Union of Tailors and Garment Workers (NUTGW) represented the two workers at the industrial tribunal.

Both claimed that they did not receive itemised pay slips; neither had been issued with written terms and conditions of employment, as was their right after 13 weeks' employment. Their representative, Barne Shuster, pointed out that Zeynep's wages were below the legal minimum rate for the clothing industry. Evidence was presented of undated wage envelopes showing false amounts; some showed no deductions at all. The tribunal condemned the treatment of the Polats, who had refused to accept fraudulent wage slips. Mehmet was awarded compensation of £4,390, plus holiday pay outstanding. Zeynep could not be awarded compensation for what the tribunal described as an 'outrageous dismissal' because she had not worked with her employer for the required 52 weeks before dismissal.

The Polats were victims of one of the most common forms of 'irregular employment' practised by unscrupulous employers.

By paying cash in hand, the employer does not pay national insurance contributions (which at the time of the Polat case stood at 13 per cent of gross pay), nor wage overheads such as sickness or holiday pay. Such employers commonly claim that their workers are either 'self employed' or 'subcontracted' to work in the factory.

If the employee agrees to be paid in this way — and often it is the only kind of work on offer — then he or she forfeits all employment protection rights and is not eligible to claim unemployment or sickness benefit. For the employers, these practices bring a double advantage: they save on wage 'extras' and the worker cannot usually challenge management, for fear of losing the job and of having to meet a large tax bill. Irregular employment therefore weakens trade unionism and reinforces low pay.

Clearly, the insecurity perpetuated by the 1971 Immigration Act is a major industrial issue for the low-paid, as significant as racial discrimination at work. None of the workers in the cases described here earns even the TUC minimum wage target of £98 per week, set early in 1984. Yet it cannot be argued that their jobs are unskilled, whether done by women or men. If the jobs are underrated, why? If employers are given the freedom to exploit the low-paid, how can wages and working conditions be improved? The next three chapters discuss some unionisation struggles amongst low-paid workers.

3. 'The mop'

In this chapter we look at the trade union organisation of one migrant community — Latin Americans working in the cleaning industry. They, like many other migrants, have come to this country primarily as work permit holders, or as political refugees in the wake of military coups. Coming to Britain to work means escaping persecution, unemployment or poverty wages, and being able to send at least some earnings home to family and friends. The contract-cleaning industry has emerged as a significant employer of migrant and immigrant workers in the past five years, mainly because of its rapid growth and thirst for cheap labour. The industry has greatly benefited from the decisions by the government and Conservative-controlled local authorities to contract-out many of their cleaning services. Firms operating central government contracts are no longer bound by the minimum rates of parliament's 'Fair Wages' resolution, and are now competing in exactly the same labour market as the rest of the contract-cleaning industry. Contract tendering, usually undertaken on an annual basis, is highly competitive. The industry is so labour intensive that the wage bill may be 80 per cent of turnover. Consequently, the price of any tender is largely dictated by the price of labour. Often, the most advanced piece of technology is a mop. The contractors' demand for workers on low wages — sometimes at a moment's notice to meet the urgent needs of a client — has drawn many migrant workers and women to the industry.

Even at a time of high unemployment, companies find it hard to attract regular indigenous labour whilst social security benefits protect people from being compelled to work at any price. Yet some migrant workers or refugees may not be entitled to claim state benefits because of their immigration status, or may be unaware of their rights even if they are entitled to claim. Others may have a full-time job which is so badly paid that they have to take an early morning or evening cleaning job to help make ends meet. They may be paid in cash, off the books. The turnover is high and the cleaners may never meet the full-time staff in the department store or office which they clean after hours. Despite such obstacles to unionisation, Latin Americans have managed to develop their own organisation within contract.

A community organises

Some of those who have been most actively involved — Juan, Rigo, Afonso and Ilenia — spoke about their experiences. Juan recalls:

> In Colombia, I was involved in the teachers' trade union movement. I had national involvement through the teachers' strike. Five thousand teachers were sacked, I was one. I continued doing things for the trade union movement until the moment when I knew I had to leave. I was facing problems with the secret police, with threats to my family because of my trade union activities.
>
> So I came here — and faced many problems. Long hours, bad pay, working Sundays. We worked without any rights at all. There was discrimination, and many other workers were in the same position. I worked in six places without being able to do anything regarding organisation. Nobody knew the procedure to defend ourselves. When we first asked for something the boss threatened to call the police or immigration, and stopped us asking for our rights.
>
> I saw the need for organising workers, but I didn't know where to go. Then we had the opportunity to meet others from our Latin American community through North Kensington Law Centre. We met at the '510' community centre in Paddington.

> We started by saying we need an *amnesty* for 'illegal' workers. But we didn't belong to any trade union movement or to the Labour Party, so no organisation could ask for us. It was very difficult to be accepted by the union bureaucracy. We needed a kind of recognition by the unions. The employers discouraged us, saying the unions were rich and wouldn't help us.
>
> We started by defending individual cases by negotiating with managers helped by our community association, the Latin American Advisory Committee. Some employers got very worried and started to respond more positively. The amount of problems dealt with by the Latin American Advisory Committee made it clear we needed a strong body organised by the workers. The majority of our community were in hotels, restaurants or cleaning jobs. Most of us had participated in the trade union movement in Colombia. We were fascinated by the possibility of joining the trade union movement in England. Someone can talk for them. It was hard at the beginning to find out where people worked, to distribute the message. But people came here to the office, and we let people know about the unionisation campaign. They spread the word round amongst other South American nationalities. Not only Latin Americans: we saw the need was for workers in general.

Ilenia joined in, pointing to some of their initial difficulties:

> There are differences between unions here and in Latin America. You can get two or three unions in one workplace in England, not so in Colombia or Chile. There will be one union in each place. There will be one main union for each industry. The best example is the miners' union in Britain.

Afonso echoed Ilenia's observation:

> When negotiations are going on it's for all the banks or the hotels. Here, it is very different. For instance, you have several unions for the teachers at different levels, but in Colombia we have one trade union, FECODE: Federacion de Educadores de Colombia.

In Latin America, too, the unions haven't been consulted by government or had a 'social contract'. It's because the government's always opposed it, more than Thatcher's government now.

Juan added:

There is still repression of the trade union movement in Colombia, so we have to organise more privately. Here, we organise openly. That feeling of fear because you belong, or because you are going to organise — that fear is still with us.

Afonso agreed:

Two or three years ago we did not know how free this country was in that respect. Could we speak freely and do these activities? We are more confident now. We knew we might lose the job — but we didn't know the impact on our personal security if we joined.

Ilenia emphasised that, in her country, trade union and political activity are very closely tied together:

We did not realise that we could do trade union work without political involvement. Many of us when we got our visas were advised to keep clear of political activities. In Chile or Colombia, if you belong to a trade union it is considered political. You can go to gaol.

Juan said it took him nearly five years to join a union in Britain. He arrived in 1975. Mainly it was because of the kind of work he was doing:

I was isolated, and my immigration status was an unauthorised worker, so I was afraid of deportation. I found an organisation after three years that was talking about the trade union movement, but it took time. We heard that the Portuguese community in London had been involved in trade union activity before.

The organisation of a union through community-based activity was described in *Hardship Hotel* by Paul Soto and Liz Dronfield:

> In 1972 a group of Portuguese hotel workers came up with a totally new approach to unionisation. Up until then, the presence of large numbers of migrant workers had always been seen as a barrier to unionisation. Migrant workers do have good reason to be afraid of joining unions. Yet within each nationality they give each other a high level of mutual support. This national solidarity provides a way of linking workers in the many diffuse establishments of the hotel industry.

The Portuguese workers belonged to a community association called the Portuguese Educational and Cultural League. Their members in the catering trade joined the Transport and General Workers Union. Other nationals joined at the same time, and the International Workers Branch of the TGWU came into being.

Juan first met the other members of his community association because of his immigration problems. They took up his case, which was eventually won. He did voluntary work for the Association. Ilenia recollects:

> There were many trade union activists here, but we didn't know where they were or how to contact them, they were just fighting for survival. And people would not accept us at first.
>
> We tried to fight an amnesty campaign, but the union movement said, 'We can't do much. You don't belong.' It took a long time to work with union and branch officials, to realise we could join and work within the union. We are not strong enough even now to organise our community and in our union to get this amnesty.
>
> Many communities are starting to do what we did three years ago. It has taken us seven years to realise that we are going to be here a long time and we have to organise ourselves at every level.

Trouble in store

Many individual problems had arisen from one large cleaning contract at a store in London's West End which employed many Latin Americans. Juan said:

> They didn't give me a holiday pay. I was sacked, they owed me money. We had 20 cases all at once there. This experience was very important because a large number of Latin Americans were working together. Secondly, our community was starting to feel fed up with all the problems: poor wages, poor conditions, harassment. They felt they could do something. And in general terms, we felt more settled, that we had some rights. Even if it was dangerous, it was time to do something.

Someone from the association went to work there, to confirm what was going on. They started to recruit people into the TGWU. Juan continued:

> We were recruiting easily one we had made the contact. The first thing was building up confidence. Sometimes it was difficult to recruit because the managers were against us. The first to join were activists in Colombia. Five or six started doing things. It needed that previous political position. They each had some kind of political or trade union experience. And they actually worked in the industries. Everyone knew you can't preach from outside. You have to be there, to work with people. It would have been difficult to organise from outside. We told the workers how important it could be if they joined. We took up some complaints, people got confidence that the union was doing things.

They recalled the company had refused to recognise the union at first, despite representations from the TGWU. But later, because of the obviously high level of membership and activity, management agreed to a ballot on union recognition. Juan described what happened:

Management came round and said, 'Vote no,' but we said, 'Leave it to the workers.' About three-quarters of the workers voted for recognition. The company accepted the verdict, and signed an agreement two months later, in March 1982. We suffered a lot of pressure. I was asked by the supervisor for my passport, 'You can't belong to the union because you are illegal here,' they said. But it was not true in my case.

Shops and office blocks offer thousands of part-time cleaning jobs, many of which are paid on a casual basis. The twilight brigades of cleaners arrive early in the morning or at night. Such jobs are a refuge for so-called 'unauthorised workers' from overseas, who may be foreign students working without permission from the Department of Employment to supplement a meagre grant. They may be 'overstayers' who have come to Britain on holiday and did not return — perhaps due to a risky political situation at home or because they preferred to have a job here, even if low paid, rather than no job at all. Or they may be 'illegal entrants' due to some technical breach of the immigration rules. Hundreds of Filipina women working in hotels and hospitals on work permits were reclassified as illegal entrants in 1979−81 by the Home Office after it won a judgement in the divisional court. The ruling stated that women who had failed to declare that they had children had no right to a work permit in the first place. Many Filipinos and workers of other nationalities who were trapped by this judgement were unaware of the work pemit regulations before they took a job in Britain. Latin Americans have suffered similar harassment.

According to *Hansard* (11 May 1983), police and immigration service officials, in a major joint-operation staged in January 1983, raided 30 private addresses in London — mainly houses in multiple occupation. They questioned dozens of residents, including many Latin Americans, in a search for people working without authorisation. The question of an amnesty is clearly an important political demand in the migrant communities. To gain wider support for this demand, such communities recognise the need to work within the unions.

Ilenia commented that some of the communities were well organised politically, but did not yet know how to transfer that knowledge and strength to organising at the trade union level. 'They have said that we have to be politically organised before going into the unions. Latin American communities are well organised at the human rights and political level, but have not yet been able to use that experience here.'

'In Britain,' said Afonso, 'we see the unions fighting for wages and holidays. In my country, we see the union as a vehicle to give power to the working people.'

Crossing the barriers

Rigo felt that there were sections in the unions that were not really cared for, like catering.

> It would be better if the low-paid were amalgamated with the rest of the workforce in a place. They are left out now. There is the old fear that the low-paid are bad to deal with because they bring salaries down. If you have a skilled labour force they don't want to open up to include the low-paid. There are some barriers in the unions against the low-paid. But many older skills are going. More workers are going to the private sector and to contract work. This mass of workers can give great support to the labour movement, if it is organised.
>
> There are barriers to organisation. What are they? First, the political inflexibility of the unions. And the industrial inflexibility of the unions. The way the union is organised — it is all right if you have skills. Then there is the issue of the tax and national insurance structure, which actually encourages moonlighting and discourages people from organising.

They recognised that union organisation in the West End store had produced better wages over the past two years, as a result of, constant representations on issues. Wages had risen ahead of inflation, though from a low starting-point. And there were still no paid holidays for part-time workers, though they could take two weeks' annual unpaid leave without losing the job.

Rigo argued that a national minimum wage would encourage union organisation in cleaning:

> It would help because it would give a bottom line. A wage people can live on would give more job security. There would be more stability in those industries. It would discourage moonlighting and all those individual practices which keep workers apart. The unions see the minimum wage as counter-productive, but for the low-paid it is not true.

Rigo claimed that it was vital to develop unionisation in contract work:

> Under present circumstances, one way to fight privatisation is to organise workers in contracting. This is the case for part-time work. As long as there is part-time work which doesn't have the same conditions as full-time work, we are divided. Part-time work is one of the most divisive things. We cannot condemn it, just make the conditions equal, so it is no longer profitable. This means we must raise the issue of women in part-time jobs and their working conditions.

As well as achieving substantial improvements in their pay and conditions, their union organisation has developed significantly in the past two years, with the union agreement extended to other cleaning contracts in the same company. Shop stewards often attend training courses. The grievance procedure is beginning to prevent unfair dismissals which would previously have taken place. Membership suffered temporary setbacks when one or two contracts were lost after the 'client' company put the cleaning work out to competitive tender.

In establishing a firm union foundation, the approach used in their early trade union work was clearly important: making contact through the community association which would then take up cases of workers unfairly treated; learning about unions and rights at work; building up self-confidence amongst would-be members; organising regular meetings in free time, usually Sundays; and producing a bilingual newsletter, *El Mopo* (*The Mop*). Various organisations played an important supporting role early on — community associations, local advice and law centres, as well as the workers' future union branch. The role of the community associations gradually fades into the background as the workers' self-organisation in the union grows in confidence.

The Latin American workers have developed their own section within their union branch, and are one of its strongest elements. Their representatives have recently discussed their unionisation methods with other communities, so sharing their experience. Because of its community origins, the section enjoys a high level of membership participation in decisions. New methods of organising such as these offer a possible way forward for low-paid workers in service industries.

4. Queensland Pleaters

The clothing industry has a long history of poor working conditions and industrial struggle. The 1906 *Sweated Trades Exhibition* had shocked public opinion by exposing the appalling exploitation of clothing workers. On the day the exhibition closed, the East End branch of the Amalgamated Society of Tailors and Tailoresses called an unofficial strike and 10,000 people marched through the streets. This action led to an official strike behind the main demand — a 12-hour day with two breaks for meals. The employers soon conceded, but the campaign also led to the creation of the trades boards by the government, which were charged with setting legal minimum rates of pay. At the time, relatively few clothing workers belonged to a trade union. Today around 40 per cent of the workforce is unionised, primarily in the National Union of Tailors and Garment Workers (NUTGW), with just under 100,000 members.

Wages are set either by union negotiations, which mainly cover workers in the larger firms, or by the wages councils, the successors to the trades boards. Neither union nor wages council has yet managed to disturb the low-wage image of the industry. So most clothing workers, especially women, are dependent on the wages council to determine their pay. Average earnings for full-time women machinists in 1983, including overtime pay, were £77.60 a week — about £10 a week below the average earnings for all women in manual jobs. The industry provides employment for some 10,000 homeworkers. About one eighth of the whole workforce is employed part time — again, the majority are women, including many who are paid less than the national insurance threshold of £34 a week (1984). In 1982, the Low Pay Unit published *From Rags to Rags* which showed that about one in every three employers is not observing the legal minimum wage rates.

In spite of these poor working conditions, union organisation is faced with various hurdles. Firms employ workers 'off the books', not paying the tax or national insurance contributions. Such arrangements undermine unionisation; firms tell their workers that the first thing the union will want is to regularise their employment position so that they will all be liable to pay arrears in their contributions — even if the employer would actually be responsible. In many small shops, workers are employed alongside the owner, making unionisation difficult, especially if management and workers are from the same community — Turkish or Bangladeshi, for example. Indeed, some workers may even be friends or relatives of the owner. Equally, women from some migrant communities are restricted from taking action independently of their husbands, because to do so would be out of keeping with their cultural traditions. Furthermore, workers in the industry still see trade unions as 'white' organisations, unrepresentative of their interests. Labour turnover in the clothing trade is about 50 per cent a year, or double the national average. Roughly 60 per cent of the workforce is employed in firms with under 20 staff. These factors make unionisation an uphill task, demanding extra union resources to service small groups of members.

An industry in decline

The free-market economics of the government have been largely responsible for a deterioration in working conditions in the industry since 1979. The total workforce has fallen by a third since that year, and now stands at around 220,000. Clothing has been in a long-term decline since the immediate postwar period, when employment was more than double today's level. Nevertheless, the industry stabilised in the late 1970s under more favourable circumstances, when the Labour government introduced strict quotas on imports and released public funds for investment, in consultation with the unions. One result was that the level of union membership in the NUTGW reached an all-time peak in 1979.

These policies were swept away in the same year. Cheap imports now flow into Britain, largely unchecked, from low-wage centres like the Philippines or Bangladesh, or from Eastern Bloc countries such as Romania, where governments subsidise exports in order to obtain foreign currency. High interest rates which marked the Thatcher government's first period of office led to many bankruptcies in an industry which relies upon borrowing to see it through slack periods. Controls on foreign exchange were lifted so that firms could invest overseas. Tootals, for example, cut their UK workforce by a third between 1975 and 1981, but their overseas employment — in Zaire and Indonesia, for instance — doubled. Now, a minority of the workers of this multinational are employed in Britain. Furthermore, the government has reduced the number of wages inspectors since 1979, so that more firms are sliding out of their obligation to observe legal minimum terms and conditions.

These factors have combined to produce working patterns increasingly like those which existed at the beginning of the century, with a proliferation of small workshops in which the wages of many workers are unprotected due to the low level of unionisation, widespread evasion of rates set by wages councils, and casual or illegal employment practices. In London, there are approximately 50,000 clothing industry workers, including homeworkers. In the East End alone, there are some 2,000 small workshops where working conditions are often appalling, as Christina testified in chapter 2.

In East London, deteriorating working conditions have met with increasing opposition from community-based organisations. Employment rights projects based in trades councils or law centres have worked with the unions, supplementing their hard-pressed resources and helping to cement relations with community organisations among the different migrant communities, Turkish or Greek Cypriot, for example. Maggie Foy, formerly with the NUTGW, said, 'For the first two years in my job as union officer I had no contact with community groups. Then, all of a sudden, there was a lot of help. With the growth of the voluntary sector came a new awareness in the community of the poor conditions.'

The strike at Queensland Pleaters came next in a line of struggles against exploitation. Here we describe the origins of this dispute, which was widely supported at the time, and then discuss the workers' views on how they had organised it.

Rules of the 'sweating' game

Queensland Pleaters is a small garment factory in Hackney. Pleating in London is a small-scale, intensely competitive business. It involves small subcontract work put out by the larger factories or West End stores. Organisation of production is straightforward: unfinished garments are contracted out to a workshop for pleating and pressing. Workers are paid on piece-rates.

The eleven staff at Queensland Pleaters included eight pleaters, one person to machine the hems, one to press garments, one packer and one driver. The eight pleaters, all men, were members of the NUTGW. Most of the staff were Turkish. Barney Shuster, area officer of the union, described some of the workers' grievances:

> One was conditions. There was a padlocked fire door, which you'll meet anywhere, but also there had been no wage increase for three years, although they had had wage cuts.
>
> One particular job, which was paying 15p an item, was cut down twice by 1p and then, the last time, by another 2p, making it 11p an item. Apparently, one worker refused to accept the price offered and was sacked, but this was before the union. The workers wanted new negotiations on piece-prices.

There were other problems. Part of the work — laying out the cloth on the cardboard pattern — was not timed so it was not paid for at all. Nor were the workers paid for the time spent hanging around at work waiting for the next job to come in. Not being paid for waiting-time is common in places where there is no union. Conversely, employees are expected to work doubly hard when the work does arrive, because as soon as employers obtain an order they want it pushed through in the shortest possible time. Then, when the next job comes in, it is measured and priced on how quickly the workers got through the work last time. This is the whole key to 'sweating' at work. The unpaid waiting-time at the beginning and end of a job is the vice in which the boss squeezes the worker tighter and tighter.

Pressed into dispute

Early in 1983, Barney Shuster met management, at the workers' request, but the owner refused to discuss their grievances direct with a union official. This would, of course, have amounted to recognising the union and the employer was only prepared to talk about grievances with the workers themselves. So the workers put their demands to management through their shop steward. Their main demands included a request to be paid for all waiting-time and higher piece-rates for difficult tasks; all panels were paid at 7½p an item, but the workers asked to receive between 8p and 11p depending on the skill required for the task. They also requested extra pay for pleating double garments. Their pay fluctuated widely because of the low piece-rates and irregular flow of work, varying between £80 and £150 a week gross. The improvements they were seeking would give them a regular wage of around £140 a week. This higher average wage would also be their holiday pay, rather than the £80 a week they normally received.

Mehmet Djemal, one of those who went on strike, said: 'We all felt the same so we said, "Let's get a better job." But I said that was no use, we had to stay and fight.' After some delay, management's sole response was to offer £16 a day for any complete day they were waiting without work. The workers knew that management would be able to find at least some work most days, so they would not easily qualify for the £16 offered. They responded by asking for the waiting-time to be paid at £2 an hour, but the company rejected this suggestion.

After discussion with their union official, six of the pleaters resolved on a token half-day stoppage of work. They sat in the factory and were ordered out. Then the employer brought out letters of dismissal. In the meantime, as they later learned, he had contacted his solicitor. The workers volunteered to return to work, to talk things over, but were not let back in. And so a protest action was turned into a strike by virtue of the hostile action of the employer.

Local support for the strike was immediate. Turkish community organisations, particularly the Union of Turkish Workers, offered support on the picket line, financial help, translations of leaflets. Indeed, some of the strikers were already active members of their community. Hackney Trades Council invited speakers to meetings, and gave financial and picket-line support. The London Central Branch of the NUTGW gave immediate financial help, and the union quickly made the strike official. Local building workers provided a Portakabin across the road for a strike office.

The strikers had estimated that about 60 per cent of their firm's work originated from a factory in Newcastle which was also organised by the NUTGW. Contacts were made with the Newcastle shop steward, who told the strikers that his members were complaining about the subcontracting of work to London, which was undercutting their own wages and depriving them of work. The Newcastle members threatened to boycott Queensland Pleaters work, so the contracting-out stopped; some of the work was returned to the parent factory uncompleted. Other suppliers of work, such as the chainstore Chelsea Girl, were contacted by the union and became concerned about the quality of work that was being produced, about delays in orders and about adverse publicity.

The strikers saw that the owner would load his van from the front to make it appear full of finished work when it left the factory. In reality, however, production ran down to a trickle, even though two of the pleaters did not support the action and additional labour was recruited. Despite the effective picket, the interruption of contracts and the considerable local sympathy for the strikers, the timing of the strike action proved to be crucial.

The workers had expected the strike to be over quickly,

especially when the Newcastle and other contracts were cancelled. But after four weeks, with no sign of management offering any compromises, the strikers decided to call their action to a halt.

The strike reassessed

In December 1983, the union arranged a meeting to discuss the lessons of the strike. Those who took part included some of the strikers, members of the Turkish community and others who had given support to the strike (including the Hackney Trades Council Support Unit). The meeting was a time to reflect on the main issues: How much solidarity had there been among the workers? What general support had they received? What account had been taken of their legal rights? How important was the timing of their action?

The discussion took place in Turkish and English. The main points were always translated and, over cups of sweet black tea, the lessons were mulled over. A striker, Salahi Ozgur, said simply: 'If all eleven of us had gone out, I'm 99 per cent sure that we would have won.' But only six of the eight union members had taken part in the industrial action. Another striker said, 'I learned two things from the strike. The first is, when we came out on strike we should all have come out. Not even one of them should stay inside. And secondly, the strikers must try really hard not to let anyone else go in. If we had done this, we would be back at work now.'

But the firm had managed to recruit other workers from the local Job Centre; several young unemployed people had been taken on. The strikers agreed that they should have made more effort to contact the unions at the Job Centre and in the Careers Offices to boycott recruitment by the firm.

'The picket was sometimes half-hearted,' said Barney. 'We needed to stagger the pickets so that you were not all on duty at once. This would have given more time to go to other union meetings, do personal things. A couple of youngsters sneaked in and got a job when you were in the hut.'

Barney thought there were two main lessons. 'Firstly, you said that you would stand and fight, for the first time in three years. That is the thing that other workers in the industry have got to do. People have got to say, "We've had enough, we're not gypsies." Otherwise there is a circular movement from place to place, and it is always downwards. Every set of workers that stands and fights stops the downward spiral.' Secondly, he felt that support for the strike had been unprecedented in the clothing industry locally. Even the press had been sympathetic. The interruption of contracts had been reasonably successful, despite the fact that it had not been prepared in advance because the workers had not expected to be dismissed.

There were lessons to be learned about the timing of the strike, too. Workers had first joined the union in February 1983. The union had asked for recognition soon afterwards, when business was still slack, and had been refused. Then the workers began to put forward their demands direct to management, just before the busy summer season opened up. This was felt to be correct timing. Subsequent delays had resulted from the employer's unwillingness to respond fairly to any of the ten proposals. A token stoppage had taken place, which, despite the approaching end of the season and the fact that less than the full workforce was unionised, was felt to have been the right decision. The employer had over-reacted and sacked all those who took part. Of course, a go-slow would have been an alternative tactic, but had that not been effective then the strikers may have looked back in regret and wished that they had actually stopped work or struck for better conditions. 'And if you go slow, you earn less money. How long can we live on that?' said Mehmet.

The workers discussed their legal rights as strikers. 'The first thing that shocked us,' said Salahi, 'was that by law they have the right to sack us, and we cannot do anything. If we had known that, we might have done something else.' The workers were under the clear impression, at the time of their stoppage, that if they were sacked they could take their employer to court. If they had appreciated the true legal position — that by striking they were breaking their contract, and therefore liable to be dismissed without the right to apply to an industrial tribunal — then some of the strikers would have preferred the option of working slowly, or some similar tactic, that allowed them to stay at work. 'He checked the law and found he could sack us,' said Mehmet. 'The work that comes in has a time limit. If it doesn't get done, then the contract folds. We could do a go-slow when an order comes in. If all eleven of us had done this we could have got away with it.'

'But,' Barney said, 'if you are going to fight by the law, you need a lawyer. If you are going to fight as workers, you need a trade union. The aim is to win control of the dispute.'

Mehmet talked about the growing competition between firms for contracts. 'There used to be a governors' agreement to do work at a certain price and they all agreed to it. Then one governor started undercutting and several went bankrupt. So you can't trust the governors to set a fair price for you.'

The workers recognised that it was difficult to establish a union in shops employing people off the books. 'Organising a union depends on the place,' said Mehmet. 'Where everything is on the books, you can get somewhere. But firms are cutting our prices. We used to get £1.20 for a shirt four years ago. Now, it is only 90p. If he gives workers their full rights, he has to close down.'

'But they are picking your pockets to survive,' responded Barney. 'Let's face it, if you organise the union properly you are bound to knock out a few smaller firms. Many only survive because they are fiddling. You need to organise in a factory that plans ahead and manages without fiddling.'

'But in those places the tax knocks people heavy,' argued Mehmet. 'You can lose £50 a week in tax and national insurance when you are working. It makes people think.'

'But when they do think,' responded Barney, 'they know that they do not get holidays or holiday pay or overtime. If you balance one against the other, you are not far down at all.'

'I want a permanent, decent job now,' said Salahi. 'It was an unhealthy place to work, a battle of nerves. I am relieved to be out of there. I was on strike in catering in 1974, in the Wimpy Bar strike. I want a decent job now, on London Transport or the council.'

The Queensland Pleaters strike had quickly attracted wide support because the local trades council and community organisations were already working actively with the NUTGW in response to deteriorating conditions in the industry. These resources had supplemented those of the union during the dispute. NUTGW membership has declined with the recession in the industry since 1979 and so, as a result, had union resources. Today, small units are emerging as the main places of employment in London, the West Midlands and elsewhere. To organise such places is especially time-consuming for the union, notwithstanding the other organisational hurdles such as turnover of labour. Clearly, the additional resources which the community had to offer helped to strengthen the position of the workers. The union itself has yet to respond by applying additional resources of its own to this section of the industry. The majority of the workforce in the garment trade are women, including many Greek Cypriot and Turkish women. Significantly, the Queensland Pleaters strikers were men. Both the union and the migrant communities need to consider recruitment and organisational strategies which would support the unionisation of women in the clothing industry.

5. Sunset on Rowton's empire

On 4 October 1983, after 14 months on the picket line, 27 strikers returned to work at Arlington House, North London, the largest men's hostel of its kind in Western Europe. Their return to work marked the end of a long dispute against the owners, Rowton Hotels plc, who, largely as the result of the strike, had sold the hostel to Camden council. It was a unique spectacle: a commercially run hostel being taken into public ownership in the Thatcher era of cuts in public spending.

The Arlington House dispute was essentially a strike against low pay, for workers in unlicensed private hostels are not protected by a wages council. Here we look at the origins of the campaign against Rowton's. We examine the organisation of the strike and some of its lessons.

Rooms for the 'deserving poor'

Arlington House, with 1,066 beds in separate cubicles, was constructed at the turn of the century by Montagu William Lowry-Corry, the first and only Lord Rowton. His intention in building this and other massive hostels which bear his name was to provide common lodging houses at a fair price, at a time when housing conditions in London were atrocious. As the author Michael Sheridan wrote in his book *Rowton Houses 1892−1954*, 'Lord Rowton was no namby-pamby charity worker. If he lent a "poor devil" money because "my conscience pricks me" he did so only after due investigation that the devil really was deserving.' It was in this spirit that Rowton provided housing for the 'deserving poor'. The expansion in the number of hostels depended on a never-ending shortage of accommodation in the capital.

In 1982, before the staff went on strike, living and working conditions had again come to resemble those of the Victorian era. The minimum working week was 48 hours, often spread over six or seven days, for which the basic pay would be as little as £26 net, plus board and lodging. Cooks and kitchen hands would work a split shift spread over 16 hours a day. Run by about 60 employees, open every day of the year, the hostel was grossly under-staffed. At that time, residents were paying £15.30 a week for a cubicle measuring only seven feet by five. There were 17 baths or showers, 93 wash-basins and 108 urinals for the 1,000 occupants. Even these limited facilities were constantly breaking down.

The cubicle size and the number of facilities were, in any case, well below the minimum levels required by Camden council. Yet Rowton's spent a tiny sum on maintenance: in 1982 Arlington House made pre-tax profits of £280,000 on a gross turnover of £860,000 that year, but only £350 was spent on repairs. There was no health and safety committee in the house. This would generally depend on a company first recognising a trade union, which Rowton's initially refused to do. The residents were also subject to Victorian disciplinary practices. For the offence of bedwetting, a resident could be fined. A typical entry in the Offences Book would be: 'Offence. Wet bed. Manager's decision £7 or VA'. 'VA' means 'vacate accommodation'. The company argued that it needed the fine to pay for the cleaning of the mattress, yet staff reported that the standard procedure was to place the mattress in a corridor by the fire escape to dry.

Management's attitude to the staff was that they were 'wayfarers', glad of a room and a job. One manager was overheard to say, 'If you can get me a man for £5 a week, then pay him £5.' Almost all the staff lived in. For them and the residents alike, the cubicles were often cold, yet many of the workers and residents were elderly.

The rate at which hostels and rooms for the single homeless have been closed down in London has created a massive shortage, perhaps as high as 10,000 bedspaces for homeless men and women. Against this background, Rowton's had itself been moving out of running hostels and into the potentially more lucrative hotel market. Their hostels at Kings Cross and at the Elephant and Castle had been converted into hotels. By 1982, the company had just four hostels left under its control — three in London (Arlington House in Camden; Vauxhall hostel in Lambeth; and Tower House in Tower Hamlets) and one in Birmingham. Similar conditions existed at these other Rowton hostels. An environmental health report produced for *Shelter* concluded that Tower House was 'unfit for human habitation'. The inspection found cisterns that did not flush, fire doors wedged open and men drinking from hosepipes. The high incidence of tuberculosis among residents had caused a major scandal in the borough. At the Vauxhall hostel in 1982, some 40 rooms were found by the local authority to be without a window and were closed down.

Working for Rowton

Bernie Jones, one of the staff who eventually went on strike, remembers his first days at the hostel. 'I was rather desperate for a job and they offered me one at £16 a week at Arlington House.' He was living at a rehabilitation centre in Lancaster, but was frustrated with not working. He called in to the local Job Centre. 'I told them I had worked at Arlington House before. The Job Centre rang Arlington House and they agreed that I could come back. I had my fare paid to Euston by the DHSS.' On arrival, he was given a brief interview, and told to start work immediately.

> The under-manager said I should take my bags upstairs to the 5s, the cubicles on the fifth floor. He gave me a set of keys and asked me to do some cleaning until the men finished the rooms. Anyone who was not as desperate as myself would have been put off by the pokey kind of accommodation.
>
> When I went to bed later on after finishing work I flung

myself on the bed and immediately the bed sagged on one side. I lifted the mattress to look at the bedstead and found it tied down one side with string. I got ready for bed. I had not been in bed above half-an-hour when I felt something crawling on my body. I ignored it for a few minutes until I started to itch. I looked at the mattress, it looked as though someone had wet the bed and it had dried and started to rot away. I peered closely at the mattress and saw little red insects scuttling about.

I went to the booking office and told them about the insects in my bed, but they told me I was lucky to have company to keep me warm. I decided to go to the staff room, which smelled strongly... I can assure you that it was not a pleasant atmosphere to spend the night in, though better than being eaten alive by insects.

Bernie described his daily routine as a bedmaker:

I went down to the vestibule where I was given a set of master keys and apportioned a landing to clean and make the beds on that landing, which had about 60 rooms. I began the day by going to every door and knocking, telling the occupant that it was gone 7.30a.m. I was told that all residents were to be out by 9.30 so that the rooms could be cleaned.

I was told to just straighten the bedclothes, but first to feel the sheets and mattresses to find if anyone had urinated in the bed. If so, I had to report it to the front office, where the name and number was put in a book. A fine was later imposed on the resident when he returned in the evening.

Agreement made and broken

On the night of 21 December 1982, one of the workers found his way accidentally into the wrong cubicle. It was empty, and he fell asleep there. The proper occupant returned some time later and reported the situation to the front office. Subsequently, a member of the night staff violently assaulted the sleeping worker, who needed hospital treatment for cuts and other injuries. Despite protests by the staff over the next few days, management took no action to discipline the night-worker.

Two weeks later, about 30 of the 60 workers walked into the nearby office of the TGWU and joined the union. 'We had secret union meetings in the house after that,' recalls Bernie Jones, 'and big meetings at the union office'. The workers' decision to join a union was encouraged by the Arlington Action Group (AAG), a group of local housing activists who had been campaigning for several years for Camden council to force Rowton's either to improve the hostel or sell it to the local authority. The AAG put the workers in contact with their local Labour MP, Jock Stallard, who also protested to the management over the assault. Within three days of the MP being involved, the assailant was arrested and charged with grievous bodily harm. He was then sacked.

Fear and anger had united the workers. By sticking together they had won a small but important victory. At a union meeting on 11 January 1982, a long list of grievances was prepared — the working week for some was 72 hours; the average wage was around £26 net; any member of staff who was too ill to work was not given the daily meal allowance; there was no clear discipline or grievance procedure; rooms were cold, the standards low. Then the meeting turned to organising the union; there would be stewards for each section of the hostel and each shift. One worker, Tom Barwise, was elected to collect the union dues each week. Members of their union branch helped to prepare a leaflet on Rowton staff grievances. The workers agreed to seek recognition of their union by the company. On 25 January a meeting took place between representatives of both sides, and a request was submitted for formal union recognition, given that a majority of the workers had joined the TGWU. Rowton's directors met and the reply came back that the board was not willing to give official recognition.

A major joint-meeting of all those concerned about the future of Arlington House took place on 16 February 1982. Those present included the majority of union members, representatives of the branch committee and Camden councillors. Hostel residents were represented by their association's committee, which was trying to establish a dialogue with the hostel management, too. Members of the local section of the Campaign for the Homeless and Rootless (CHAR) and of the AAG attended; both of these groups had a long history of supporting the residents in their attempts to win improvements at the hostel.

This meeting set out a joint strategy which would last for the duration of the campaign against Rowton. The union would deal with low wages and the appalling working conditions. Other issues in the house, especially the poor facilities and the neglect of the residents, would be taken up by their committee working with the AAG and CHAR, who would, together, put further pressure on the council to take firm action against the owners.

The main early demand of the residents was that the council should take over the hostel with a compulsory-purchase order. Reflecting the local support offered at the meeting, local councillor Hugh Bayley said, 'The whole Labour group on the council supports the union's demand for recognition.' Thus a new determination emerged on the part of the local authority to persuade Rowton's to submit serious plans either to improve the hostel or sell out. The company's immediate response to such pressure was to threaten to close the house down, thereby confronting the council with a vast rehousing responsibility. In turn, the council developed contingency plans to cope with this possible reaction by the company.

Then, on Thursday 1 April 1982, the company sacked two of the shop stewards. The first, a clerk, was suspended for allegedly accepting a booking without due authority; he was allowed to appeal. The second steward attempted to accompany the first to this appeal and was suspended. Both were then interviewed at head office and sacked, the company having refused to allow the union officer to represent either shop steward. The room of one steward, Jack Jenkinson, was broken into – but only union papers were taken.

The workers called an urgent meeting, but management refused to allow kitchen staff to attend. The meeting decided to take action if the two union representatives were not reinstated. 'There was a lot of humming and hahing,' said Bernie, 'even though the stewards were outside picketing. But the MP and local councillors and others soon came down to help.' The company refused to accept an appeal by the union for reinstatement.

In another development in the crisis, the stewards were threatened with eviction from their rooms over that weekend. The local law centre immediately wrote to the hostel manager reminding him that, under the 1977 Protection from Eviction Act, it would be a criminal offence to evict a person unlawfully, 'other than by reasonable notice and a court order'. This weekend legal intervention forestalled the eviction and held up the morale of the sacked members at a crucial time. Yet over this same weekend, another of the union representatives and three other workers and residents were assaulted by a member of the night staff.

All of these events brought the workers together. As the early shift reported for duty at 5.30a.m. on the Monday morning, the workers joined the picket line. By 8a.m. almost all the staff were on the pavement, calling for the reinstatement of the sacked stewards and the recognition of their union. The company was shaken by the display of unity shown by the workers and by early afternoon had agreed to reopen negotiations with the union, partly due to persuasion by the local MP. After some hours of talks, it was announced that the company had agreed to reinstate the sacked stewards and to allow a union recognition ballot under the supervision of the Advisory, Conciliation and Arbitration Service (ACAS). Thus, on 15 April, some 55 of the 63 staff at the hostel voted 'Yes' in reply to the single question: 'Do you wish to be represented by the Transport and General Workers Union?'

Build-up to public acquisition

Over the summer months it became clear, however, that Rowton's had no real intention of making the agreement with the union work. Few substantial improvements took place in spite of several meetings at which proposals were put forward. In June, the workers drew up a list of demands: a 40-hour week, a £20 wage rise, at least one full day of rest a week, no shift to exceed 12 hours, uniforms to be provided by the company and the food allowance not to be withdrawn when a worker was absent sick. Though the proposals would be costly, they would still only result in a basic wage of about £70 a week, including board and lodging.

In response, the company first of all delayed meeting the union; when a meeting did take place, in September, management declared that the union agreement only covered individual grievances, not negotiations on pay. The workers reacted angrily to this statement, demanding immediate talks on conditions in the hostel. When these were again refused, they walked out. This time Rowton's ordered them back to work, and sacked them all when they refused to comply. Even a delay by the union in declaring the strike 'official' failed to persuade the employer to de-escalate the conflict and permit a return to work.

The strike began on 9 September 1982 and was to last through until October of the following year. The reason for the new hard line by Rowton's emerged three weeks after the strike began: the company suddenly announced that it intended to sell its four remaining hostels. The asking price was £6 million. Despite a major campaign involving the picketing of the company's other hostels and hotels in London, the workers did not succeed in bringing Rowton's back to the negotiating table. Initially, the strikers had looked to workers in the other hostels to join them in sympathy action. Women cleaners at the Vauxhall hostel enlisted in the union straightaway, but the men working in this and other hostels would not take supporting action — primarily because they also feared the sack and eviction.

During the year of the dispute, the union undertook extensive negotiations with the local authorities which were trying to acquire the hostels, mainly to ensure that the purchases went through as quickly as possible. The fact that the sale of Arlington House was tied up with the disposal of the other two hostels in London meant that the negotiations were complex, though matters were greatly simplified when the Greater London Council began to co-ordinate affairs in December. Two further developments assisted this process: the GLC decided to buy Tower House on behalf of the local council which was reluctant to add such a hostel to its housing stock; and Lambeth council returned to Labour control after a by-election, so that all the London authorities concerned were then under Labour administrations. Camden council agreed to a request by the union that it would re-employ all the strikers if it were to buy the hostel.

In the middle of negotiations with the local authorities, Rowton's let it be known that it was considering a deal with a private developer. The hostels would be sold with vacant possession if it went through, and some 2,200 men were likely to be made homeless. Valuations of the hostels undertaken by the councils had arrived at a total figure of less than half Rowton's asking price; the councils were not permitted to bid above these values. In some desperation, local MPs petitioned the housing minister to intervene. In response, the government proposed that it would be prepared to sanction the local authority purchase of the hostels if they and Rowton's would agree to abide by the decision of an independent valuer. Rowton's reluctantly agreed to this compromise. Eventually, in June 1983, the company's shareholders met and resolved to accept an offer of £2,930,000 for the three London buildings. The same meeting voted the chairman and two directors off the board.

Working together

The union branch, the local Labour Party, the council and the AAG played important roles in helping the strikers maintain a picket line for months on end. Alternative accommodation was required after 30 November, when Rowton evicted the 45 remaining strikers. The mass eviction was supervised by hundreds of police and opposed by an equally large demonstration. From then on, the council and local housing associations housed the strikers; the Labour Party offered a local office with a kitchen for hot meals, and meeting and rest facilities. Their union launched two main financial appeals; many other unions and political groups gave donations and assisted with picketing and boycotting supplies. The strike committee drew up lists of suppliers, some of whom were unionised — initially, the picket line substantially interrupted Rowton's business affairs, though the effect faded as they turned to alternative, non-union sources.

By the autumn of 1983, the transactions were completed and the hostels sold into the public sector. Though now owned by Camden council, Arlington House is managed for them by United Kingdom Housing Trust. Local authorities own and manage the two other London hostels. The number of workers employed in the three hostels has risen from about 140 to nearly 200, and a £4 million programme of modernisation has been initiated, making up for years of neglect. During the summer of 1983, the union entered into negotiations with the UKHT on new terms and conditions of employment. When the Arlington House strikers returned to work their minimum wage was £105 for a 36-hour week, working conditions had improved in every respect and they were covered by a union recognition agreement with the new employer. Camden council had indeed kept to its early assurance that all the strikers would be re-employed.

The strikers won their dispute because of their own determination, combined with the reliable local support which they received throughout. They had exposed the appalling conditions in the house; many organisations rallied to their cause. The local authorities had perhaps allowed Rowton's too much latitude in trying to persuade it to modernise the conditions in the hostels. The unionisation of the workforce was a new factor which almost certainly propelled the company into the decision to sell out. Yet if Labour administrations had not been in control of the boroughs and the GLC, it is far less likely that the hostels would have ended up in the public sector. The hostel in Birmingham, where the council was under Conservative direction, was sold privately.

6. Trade union law

In recent times, low-paid workers have often been engaged in bitter disputes for union recognition and basic rights — at Grunwicks and Garners Steak Houses, at Aire Valley Yarns and Imperial Typewriters, as well as those described in the preceding chapters of this book. Frequently, they have included migrant and immigrant workers — women as often as men — in clothing, catering and new small-scale manufacturing industries. These examples all point to the determination of workers in low-wage industries to unionise. But they also demonstrate their mixed fortunes in doing so.

The problem has been made worse by the Tory government's weakening or repeal of laws designed to protect people at work. Many of these protections were curtailed by the 1980 Employment Act. It is now a much more difficult and risky business for workers to organise. Rising unemployment in fact heightens the need for employment protection, to prevent employers from crudely dismissing workers because 'there is always someone else who will do the job if you don't want to.' Precisely because many low-paid workers do not have the protection of a union agreement (especially if they work in a small establishment), they have been hardest hit by the erosion of basic rights at work. All of these changes are aimed at increasing the insecurity of labour, allowing employers greater freedom to hire and fire, extracting the maximum output for the least wages.

The purpose of this chapter is to look at the practical effects of the government's policy for workers trying to win union recognition. The two key issues are the rights of individual union members who begin to organise at work, and the collective rights of a group of members seeking union recognition.

Protecting the individual activist

In the autumn of 1982, two workers in a hotel in Maida Vale, London, began to encourage the 60 staff to join the Transport and General Workers Union. One activist, Carmen, was a chambermaid who had been employed at the hotel for about two months when the hotel was sold. The new company, Verani, immediately introduced a package of economy measures without consulting the staff. The number of rooms to be serviced by each chambermaid daily was increased by 25 per cent, from 12 to 15 rooms, with no increase in the hourly rate of pay of £1.65. Staff in various departments were summarily dismissed.

Within a fortnight, about half of the workers had joined the union, many for the first time in their working lives. Meetings took place between management and the two active union members, although the company saw them as individuals and not as 'union representatives'. The representatives were under the impression that at least some of the grievances would be dealt with seriously. Both workers attended a shop steward induction course organised by their union over the next weekend, expecting to meet the hotel manager again on the following Tuesday.

On Monday morning, however, Carmen was dismissed: management alleged that she had been late for work, though she had in fact been given permission by her head of department to attend a hospital appointment. She was told to leave her job immediately and to leave her staff accommodation by Friday. The other active member, a porter, was given a final written warning for lateness. He believed that he, too, would have been sacked but for his longer service of two years with the company. He had never been pulled up for lateness before.

Despite appeals from her fellow-workers and the union officer, management refused to reinstate the chambermaid or to withdraw the porter's final warning letter. At this point, there were two options open to union members: to take industrial action or try further negotiations. As new union members, fearful of the sack and with their representatives under attack, they proposed that their union official should try to resolve the crisis through further negotiation with the employer, using whatever legal and other pressures could be applied.

Carmen did not have the legal right to make a standard appeal to an industrial tribunal for 'unfair dismissal' because she had not completed the necessary period of continuous service. In October 1979, the Conservatives had doubled the qualifying period of service (laid down in the 1978 Employment Protection Consolidation Act) from 26 to 52 weeks. Even under the old rules, she had not worked at the hotel long enough to make a standard unfair dismissal claim. However, Carmen could have made a specific appeal for unfair dismissal for her trade union membership or activities. This is described as an 'interim relief' appeal under Section 77 of the Act, for which there is no qualifying period of service.

There are two significant problems with claims for unfair dismissal for trade union activities. First, the process is slow and complex. Only an official of a registered trade union can make an application to the tribunal on behalf of the member. The appeal must be lodged within seven days of the dismissal, but even a preliminary hearing of the evidence may take several weeks to arrange; the full hearing, in keeping with the general run of unfair dismissal cases, may be delayed even further. Second, the 1980 Employment Act shifted the burden of proof in *all* unfair dismissal claims away from the employer. Where there is a straight conflict of evidence in a case, the employer once had to prove that he or she acted reasonably in sacking the worker. Since the 1980 Act, the tribunal must come to a decision on whom to believe. In practice, it is rare for a straight conflict of evidence to be resolved in favour of the employee. This situation owes much to the fact that an employer is more likely to be legally represented than a worker, for legal aid is not available at industrial tribunals.

Carmen also had the right not to be unlawfully evicted from her staff accommodation, under Section 1(2) of the 1977 Protection from Eviction Act. Her occupation of the room in staff quarters could not be terminated without reasonable notice, usually meaning at least 28 days, followed by a court order if necessary. Employers trying to evict staff are obliged to follow these procedures, though many workers in tied accommodation do not realise that they have this protection.

Carmen's management was threatened with both a court injunction if it tried to evict her forcibly, and with an 'interim relief' appeal to a tribunal if she was not given her job back. But management refused to reinstate her. Moreover, the tribunal case appeared to be unreliable because of the short period of Carmen's service at the hotel and the reason given for her dismissal — lateness. It would also have required evidence from one of the management to support her claim that she had permission to attend hospital. Because of the pressure she was under, Carmen felt that her best course of action was to ask the union official to seek a settlement with the employer. At the end of the week, she left the hotel with £225 compensation, with the employer paying for weekend accommodation in another hotel. Unfortunately, the other union activist, who had drawn a lot of his enthusiasm from his sacked colleague, then resigned from the hotel in disgust. Some weeks later, though, two other workers volunteered to continue to try to organise the union there.

Many trade unionists believe that going to a tribunal is virtually an admission of defeat at the workplace. For aggrieved trade union members, the failure rate for their complaints to tribunals is phenomenal. Between 1979 and 1982, only one in every six appeals was successful. Some 2,257 complaints were made by sacked trade unionists, resulting in 291 voluntary settlements and just 106 successful tribunals — a total of just 397 positive results (see Table 5), so that just one in every six appeals was successful.

The 1980 Employment Act

The 1980 Employment Act was a major part of the government's strategy to 'redress the balance' between the 'powerful' trade unions and employers. Yet, ironically, it is the isolated individual worker without union representation at work who has been worst affected by it. The Act introduced a new stage into the tribunal procedures, the 'pre-hearing assessment'. Tribunals now look at the preliminary evidence available; on the basis of this information, applicants may be warned by the tribunal that if they pursue the case and lose, costs may be awarded against them.

Table 5 Dismissal of trade union members: 1979 to 1982

Year	Complaints made	Voluntary settlements	Tribunal hearings	Complaints upheld
1979	545	50	263	33
1980	621	140	255	34
1981	271	48	82	18
1982	820	53	126	21
Total	2,257	291	726	106

Source: *Hansard*, 28 October 1983.

Hundreds of cases have been withdrawn each year as a result of this new procedure. It is bound to deter workers, who are not entitled to legal aid representation by a solicitor and may be suddenly involved in meeting unfamiliar officials and making difficult decisions on their own. Yet, in cases where a warning has been issued by the tribunal, workers have still gone on to win at a full hearing. On the other hand, in 1981, the first year when full statistics were available, tribunals made 235 awards of costs in unfair dismissal cases; of these, 229 were against workers, 6 against employers. In no less than one-quarter of these cases, no prior warning had been given by the tribunal that costs might be made against an unsuccessful party.

As we have seen, the Act also shifted the burden of proof in support of unfair dismissal cases away from the employer. The combined result of these changes has been to reduce further the effectiveness of tribunals as places where workers might obtain some redress against arbitrary management. In 1982, 33,109 unfair dismissal claims were made to industrial tribunals. Almost two-thirds of these (21,600) were taken up by ACAS, which arranged voluntary conciliation between the employer and employee. Only 421 workers were re-engaged. This left 11,509 cases which proceeded to a tribunal hearing, where 70 per cent (7,974 cases) were lost by workers. In those which were successful, only 136 workers were rewarded with reinstatement. So a grand total of 557 sacked workers won their claim for unfair dismissal *and* were re-engaged. This is about 16 out of every 1,000 original applications. One of the primary aims of the 1975 Employment Act was to assist workers to achieve *reinstatement* if they were unfairly sacked, for whatever reason. For the one in three tribunal applicants who won their case, financial compensation was the main reward — though in 1982, around half of workers to whom an award was made received less than £400.

Second-class workers

The 1980 Employment Act also ruled that those employed in small workplaces with 20 staff or less, would have to complete two years service before they could qualify to claim for unfair dismissal. Under previous regulations, the qualifying period had been 26 weeks, the same as for workers in larger establishments.

In *Striking a Balance?* Roy Lewis and Bob Simpson assessed employment law after the 1980 Act. They estimated that some four million people were employed in small workplaces, or roughly one-sixth of the working population. The government, with it much professed belief in supporting small entrepreneurs, justified the change in the law on the grounds that small firms were reluctant to take on new workers because Labour's laws had made it difficult to dismiss them later on. Yet business surveys found that there were far more significant explanations of small firms' reluctance to recruit staff — lack of finance for business expansion and high interest rates were more salient than employment protection rights. In 1978, before the rules were changed, it was estimated that a quarter of all unfair dismissal claims came from workers in firms with 20 workers or less; small employers were statistically more likely to be found guilty of sacking a worker unfairly. Labour's employment protection legislation did not stop dismissals so much as encourage employers to treat their staff with greater respect and introduce greater fairness into disciplinary prodedures.

Part-time workers were given some safeguards under the 1975 Employment Protection Act. After five years' service with the same firm, those working between 8 and 15 hours a week could qualify for the right to claim unfair dismissal. Many observers now consider that this period of service is excessively long; the 1980 Employment Act simply failed to shorten the qualifying period. There are approximately 4.5 million part-timers in Britain, working 30 hours a week or less, the majority of whom are women.

Furthermore, there is a growing trend in the service industries to take on casual workers. The 60 casuals sacked by Trust House Forte at the Grosvenor House Hotel, London, in 1983, appealed to an industrial tribunal and were represented by their union, the General, Municipal, Boilermakers and Allied Trades Union (GMBATU). But the tribunal ruled that they were not 'employees' in the meaning of the 1975 Employment Protection Act, so they did not have the right to claim thay they were unfairly dismissed. Some of the workers had been 'casuals' at this hotel for the best part of their working lives. The GMBATU is taking this case to the European Court.

The 1980 Employment Act and the increasing practice of employing people on a casual or part-time basis, are together creating a vast group of second-class employees — 'legally unprotected workers' — with no legal defence against arbitrary dismissal.

Recognition rights removed

The 1980 Employment Act also abolished statutory procedures which had helped workers to obtain union recognition. Workers in Britain have never had the legal *right* to union recognition itself. But Labour's employment legislation in 1975 and 1978 set out procedures, involving ACAS, to encourage and persuade employers to meet with union representatives rather than turn away from them. All of these procedures were abolished in August 1980. The workers in the case of the Maida Vale Hotel therefore no longer had access to statutory processes to assist their claim for recognition. In the first instance, under Section 11 of the 1978 Employment Protection Consolidation Act (EPCA), the advisory services of ACAS were expected to achieve a voluntary settlement between trade union and employer over union recognition. But the EPCA also gave ACAS the power to investigate the level of support in a firm if it would not readily agree to accept the union. This might have involved a ballot of workers under Section 12 of the Act and the publication of a report by ACAS with recommendations as to the way forward. If an employer refused to accept an ACAS recommendation that the union be recognised for the purpose of collective bargaining, then that union could, under Section 16 of the EPCA, proceed to submit a further claim for improvements in the wages and conditions of members. Such a claim would be heard by the Central Arbitration Committee (CAC). Any award made by the CAC was in fact binding on the employer, since the new terms and conditions were included in the contract of employment of the workers concerned. The CAC had stopped short, however, of ruling that the right to union representation should be one of the new terms in a worker's contract.

During the life-span of Sections 11 to 16 of the EPCA, approximately 65,000 workers achieved recognition as a direct result of the statutory procedures. A total of 1,610 recognition claims were received by ACAS, the majority from small and medium-size firms. Roughly 16,000 workers in 247 of these firms obtained recognition only after the full legal procedures were used. Trade unions looked upon the stages of the EPCA more as something in reserve, not the first line of approach to an employer. Both sides knew that the union was likely to activate statutory procedures if direct negotiations broke down. Between 1975 and 1979, trade union membership in Britain increased by about 1,101,000, reaching a peak of 12,702,000 members in that year. So approximately 6 per cent (65,000) of the net growth over the period was attributable directly to the processes set out in the EPCA. Though these statistics are only an estimate, they suggest that ACAS played onlhy a small immediate part in the growth of collective bargaining.

ACAS and the EPCA helped to create a climate which encouraged union growth, good employment practices and a greater willingness by employers to talk to their workers through union representatives. The repeal of the EPCA procedures has certainly helped to stem the flow of new union agreements since 1980, so that unions have found it more difficult to replace agreements lost due to the closure of firms which once negotiated with them. Increasing numbers of employers, in the leisure industries, for example, are terminating existing agreements with recognised unions.

Yet when the statutory assistance to trade union development was abolished in 1980, the unions raised only a token voice of protest. A minority of firms had so frustrated the operation of the Act that unions had become entangled in unwanted local battles. Though there was no right of appeal against an ACAS recommendation, its role in the recognition process was undercut by a series of court decisions founded on the allegation that it had exceeded its statutory powers. In the case of the long-running Grunwick strike (1976−7) the majority of the workforce, including many immigrant women workers, walked out on strike to protest against being pressed too hard by their employer for meagre rewards. They demanded that the firm recognise their union and improve working conditions. ACAS was duty-bound to assess the level of support for the union amongst the whole workforce, including those who had not come out on strike. However, the firm refused to provide ACAS with their names and addresses, so when the service produced a report based on the views of those whom it could consult, recommending union recognition, the employer appealed on the grounds that it had not fulfilled it statutory duty. Eventually, the case reached the House of Lords, which upheld the employer's claim and declared that ACAS should have consulted all sections of the workforce, not just those on strike. One Law Lord described the ACAS procedures as 'an interference with individual liberty' − meaning the liberty of an employer to recognise a union, regardless of workers' opinions.

In its 1979 annual report, ACAS stated that 'it could not satisfactorily operate the statutory procedures as they stand' because of the extent to which the courts and employers together were frustrating the work of the service. Some of the obstructive behaviour by employers could have been overcome by relatively simple improvements to the EPCA, which might, for example, have given ACAS more leeway in its duties to consult with workers. Before the 1979 general election, some Labour MPs argued that workers should be able to make an unfair dismissal claim if they had been sacked for striking in support of a recommendation by ACAS which their employer was refusing to comply with.

Before the 1980 Employment Act, companies which were in dispute with their workers were penalised if they tried selectively to re-employ some strikers but not others − the activists, for example. Under Section 62 of the EPCA, those not taken back at the end of a dispute could take their firm to a tribunal, claiming unfair dismissal. The Employment Act repealed this right: employers may now freely induce some strikers to return, and have no fear of industrial tribunal claims from those left out in the cold.

Before the abolition of this right took effect, in December 1982, workers at a restaurant in central London fought a three-week strike for union recognition in which the employer's wish not to take back certain strikers was put to the test. At this restaurant, the staff had unsuccessfully submitted various grievances to management over the summer of 1981: an annual pay rise, due in July, had not been paid; new waiting staff were being taken on at 30p an hour less than the existing workers; tips wre being used to justify low basic rates. At least half the workers joined a union within a few weeks; management refused to recognise it. They agreed instead to discuss some of the grievances directly with the workers, but then arguments broke out over the minutes of these meetings. Then, in December 1981, two of the union representatives, who had played an active part on the staff committee, received written warnings for alleged lateness and misconduct. The unionised workers saw this as an attack on their organisation. When management refused requests to withdraw the letters, the union members walked out in protest and formed a picket on the pavement outside. Customers began to turn away. The company ordered the staff to return, threatening them all with dismissal. As the warnings had not been withdrawn, however, the workers refused to accept this ultimatum and all 35 were sacked.

The strike lasted three weeks over a cold, snowy Christmas and New Year. The trade in the restaurant was so badly hit by the dispute that the company agreed to enter into talks with the union around a return to work. These discussions were overseen by ACAS. The key sticking-point was the company's refusal to take back some staff, including one of the shop stewards. The strikers refused to be divided in this way. The company's plan was doubly confounded by the high level of compensation that those not taken back could have been awarded at an industrial tribunal. Faced with these arguments, the firm decided that all those on strike should be reinstated. Then, as agreed, the warning letters were put through a new appeals procedure, with indifferent results. The unionised staff, though, strengthened by the dispute, persuaded the proprietors to agree to a ballot on union recognition. A majority voted for the union and an agreement was signed in July 1982.

Cutting through the jungle: new union rights

There were three main shortcomings of the recognition procedures repealed by the government. First, separate procedures dealt with workers' *collective* attempts at union recognition (referred to ACAS) and the protection of sacked trade union *members* (referred to industrial tribunals). Second, ACAS was expected to play a dual role, both persuading and, if that failed, compelling the employers to co-operate with the unions. By 1979, ACAS had reached the conclusion that these two functions could not both be carried out by one and the same body. Third, the powers of arbitration, though not heavily used, stopped short of giving the workers the collective right to be represented by their union.

Because of such failings, the government's decision to abolish the controversial recognition procedures was not forcefully condemned by the TUC at the time; privately, many unions were glad to see the back of them. Nonetheless, for many low-paid, under-unionised workers today, the right to be represented by their union is a vital issue. New procedures might prove valuable, especially to groups of low-paid workers, if based firmly on the right to arbitration over their claim for recognition. Such procedures should also offer greater protection to individual workers facing dismissal for their union activities. The following imaginary situation, involving a number of workers whose employer has just refused to recognise their union, shows the kind of procedures needed.

In this situation, the union might initially have the right to refer its claim to a future Industrial Arbitration Board. To protect the trade union members, the board would then automatically serve a 'protected employees' notice' on the firm, which would be advised that all its staff qualified for protection against unfair dismissal, whether full- or part-time, regardless of their length of service. This notice might also declare that the only admissible reason for dismissal would be gross misconduct. Appeals would be heard within three days of dismissal by a standing tribunal; the burden of proof would, once again, be on the firm to show that it had acted reasonably. The normal remedy for any unfair dismissal would be an order for the reinstatement of the sacked worker. The collective recognition claim might then be referred to a conciliation body, such as ACAS, for a brief period in which a voluntary settlement might be worked out. If conciliation should fail, the union could then return to the board for arbitration on its appeal. The two sides would then be called together and each would be given the opportunity to present evidence on union membership, wages and conditions and any other relevant factors. Following this, the board would arbitrate on the workers' claim for recognition and for fair wages. To enforce the decision, the board might have the authority to introduce collective rights into individual worker's contracts of employement — for instance, the right to be represented by the union at shop steward and official level within the firm's grievance and disciplinary procedure. Refusal by an employer to honour an arbitration award would amount to a breach of contract and would be legally enforceable by civil court action. If the board did not have the authority to arbitrate in this way, then it would be operating a 'fair wages' procedure — not one designed to assist workers to obtain union recognition.

So far, workers have never received adequate statutory support for their union recognition claims, however powerfully the labour movement may have otherwise backed particular campaigns. New measures of this kind are required, since experience shows how effective anti-union practices by management can be. As the government cuts back employment and union rights, so the laws of the free-market jungle take over. By the late 1980's, with the monetarist-inspired growth of the low-wage sector in the economy, trade union rights will have become a critical issue.

7. Wage protection

The government claims that 'wage regulations' of various kinds, such as the wages councils' minimum rates of pay, have 'priced workers out of jobs' by setting wages at artificially high levels, especially for the lowest-paid. This is based on the idea that wage regulations are an interference with the 'free market' for labour. They have to be abolished, argue the monetarists, so that market forces alone can decide what wage levels should be. Just how far wages should be allowed to fall once all the controls are removed, given mass unemployment, is not made clear. But the government has set about destroying wage regulations with the same resolute approach it has taken towards the dismantling of workers' rights and collective bargaining by the unions.

In a debate on low pay in the House of Commons in March 1983, a Treasury minister described the government's intentions in the following way: 'We were conscious of the need to make changes in the operation of the labour market, where we wanted to eliminate unnecessary rigidities.'

Wage regulation has been attacked by the government in three main ways. First, by the abolition in September 1983 of the 'Fair Wages' resolution of parliament. This measure ensured that workers employed on central government contracts enjoyed wages and conditions no less favourable than those agreed by the unions in the particular industry, or failing that, no lower than the general level of pay for the trade. Second, the government threatens to scrap wages councils in 1985. These bodies set legally enforceable minimum wages, holidays and certain other conditions for almost three million workers in the private sector.

Third, government schemes for young, unemployed workers aged 16 and 17 are based upon cheap wage rates. The government's regulations covering these programmes include wages which are often far below the level negotiated by unions in the industry or those set by the relevant wages council. Because of their importance for the low-paid, we examine these three issues in detail here.

'Fair Wages' abandoned

Parliament's 'Fair Wages' resolution was formally abolished by the government on 22 September 1983. In scrapping the 'Fair Wages' clause, the government broke with a time-honoured parliamentary tradition — that by resolution of the House of Commons, firms operating any contract for central government, should offer fair wages and conditions to their staff.

The Low Pay Unit's *Back to the Sweatshops* describes the origins of the 'Fair Wages' clause in government contracts: 'The first resolution was introduced in 1891 under a Conservative government, with the unanimous support of the House of Commons, as a means of combating "the evils recently disclosed before the Sweating Committee".' Not that this first resolution was adequate. Attainment of reasonable conditions took years of working-class protest and the major propaganda effect of the 1906 national *Sweated Trades Exhibition* (which, according to the *Daily News*, covered all the sweated trades, 'from trouser-making to bible-folding, from jumping jacks and mouse traps to babies bibs'). Then, in 1909, under the guidance of Winston Churchill, President of the Board of Trade in the Liberal government, a much strengthened 'Fair Wages' resolution (FWR) was introduced, covering hours and conditions of work, as well as pay. The resolution was renewed after the Second World War. In a 1946 Commons debate, Harold Macmillan, speaking from the Opposition benches, described the FWR as a protector 'of the standards of living of the workers'. He added: 'It was the Treasury bench, the people inside the Treasury, who were always scrapping to see whether they could obtain some small advantage by placing their contracts at some slightly lower price with some second- or third-rate contractors.'

Thus, the purpose of the resolution was to protect workers from exploitation, to defend responsible contractors from unfair undercutting of wages by 'cowboy' competitors and to ensure a reasonable standard of work. It ensured that wage rates on cleaning or catering contracts, for example, were set at the same level as those of local authority manual workers in the same jobs.

All-party support for the resolution ran in a straight line until Norman Tebbit, as secretary of state for employment, arranged for its abolition in September 1983. He argued the exact opposite of Macmillan's case. The terms of the FWR were an 'imposition' on central government. By this he meant that they interfered with the government's right to allow the market to determine wage levels in government contracts. It is certainly true that abandoning the resolution means massive savings in the cost of government contracts. It is also vital to the government's programme of 'privatising' the health service and other public services: at the same time as they are put out to private contract, the bill for wages, holidays, absence through sickness and other conditions of employment is cut. Massive savings in public expenditure are made on both existing and on new private contracts. On every occasion, it is the low-paid who make these cuts possible with their reduced conditions of employment.

Enter the 'cowboy' contractors

The main cleaning contractors have been shaken by the government's decision on the FWR, which they believe will result in fierce wage undercutting by competitors. These leading firms are members of the Contract Cleaning and Maintenance Association (CCMA). At the time the resolution was abolished, the CCMA met the government health minister for consultations on seeking tenders for cleaning and catering contracts in the health service. The CCMA was worried about the removal of the clause governing minimum terms and conditions, and subsequently wrote to the minister, stating:

> The CCMA believes that all future public-sector tenders for cleaning and maintenance should include minimum terms

for employees. The advantages would include reducing trade union resistance to the changes [and] discouraging so-called cowboy contractors.

The CCMA pointed out that allegations from workers that contractors were paying excessively low wages could be very damaging, bringing the plans to denationalise the health service into disrepute. The employers' plea fell on deaf ears. Now that the FWR has gone, there is no form of wage regulation for cleaners working for private contractors, for there has never been a wages council covering this industry. A senior director of one of the top three companies said:

> On the CCMA there is no unity about having a wages council. There are about six first-division contractors and 200 in the fourth division, so each contract is like a cup final. If I go to a contract which is up for renewal and I start talking about increasing the wages to keep up with inflation, they start talking about putting the contract out to tender again.

His view on the government's decision was that 'it is actively forcing down wages. It is not being passive, merely revoking the "Fair Wages" clause.'

The main contractors feel vulnerable without the FWR. To illustrate the point, the director described a recent experience over a small private cleaning contract:

> Some of us got together to put in tenders for a contract in Surrey. We had a talk and agreed that the hourly rate should be £1.60. We all went away, did our calculations and put in our bids. The one who got it put in at £1.40. He had gone back to his boss, who instructed him not to go along with the gentlemen's agreement.

This kind of unscrupulous wage undercutting is now returning to government contracting for the first time since the beginning of the century. The principal firms lend their support to the idea of a voluntary national minimum wage rate, and would be prepared to consult with the trade unions on it. Though this agreement would not include holidays and other conditions of employment, it would help to stave off the worst of the undercutting practices which are now a serious problem in the industry. In 1981, ACAS published a report on the industry which found that wages were low and union organisation weak; it recommended that a wages council should be set up to regulate conditions of employment. This report has been shelved by the government, because to implement the recommendations would be to contradict its own decision on the FWR.

Will the abolition of the FWR achieve its main aim of pricing people back into work? The chair of Brengreen Holdings, which controls the large Exclusive Cleaning group, 'doubted, as others did, that the cuts would lead to more workers being employed. In the short term, there could be fewer jobs' (*Financial Times*, 20 October 1983). One option open to cleaning firms will obviously be to reduce costs by increasing labour-productivity, by sacking some workers and increasing the workload of the rest.

The threat to wages councils

The government would like to abolish wages councils and the legal minimum wage rates which they set every year. In a Commons debate in July 1982, Norman Tebbit, then secretary of state for employment, asked,

> Is there really a case for wages councils imposing minimum rates that frustrate market forces? In my opinion, any reasonably minded man must come to the same conclusion as my right honourable and learned friend. To put it mildly, the answer to the question would appear to be 'No'.

The 1983 Conservative election manifesto declared: 'We shall continue to ensure that wages councils do not reduce job opportunities by forcing workers to charge unrealistic pay rates, or employers to offer them.' John Selwyn Gummer, in a debate in the House of Commons on low pay in February 1984, continued the attack: he would 'face squarely the problems posed by wages councils'. Workers would appreciate his efforts to save them from asking unrealistically high wages.

About 1,180,400 workers are covered by the three wages councils in the hotel and catering industry. In January 1984, as Mr Gummer spoke, the highest legal minimum rate was £76.84 a week for a club steward in London. The main reason why wages councils have not yet been scrapped is because their existence is protected by an International Labour Organisation Convention on low pay, to which Britain is a signatory. Indeed, Britain was a founder-member of the ILO. Convention 26 requires member states to set up machinery for fixing minimum rates of pay in industries where wages are low and where 'no arrangements exist for the effective regulation of wages by collective bargaining'. This Convention is due to expire in 1985, when Britain will have the opportunity to renew its support, or not. The government, meanwhile, has taken various steps to undermine wages councils, or at least to wilfully neglect them.

Below the baseline
Since 1979, the number of employers who have been found not to be observing the legal minimum rates set by wages councils has risen considerably. The proportion of establishments where wages inspectors found underpayment rose from 31 per cent of places inspected in 1979 to nearly 40 per cent in 1982. One of the main reasons for this increase in the crime rate is the cut in the number of inspectors by one-third since the government first took office. Now, just 119 officers are responsible for 400,000 workplaces registered under the different wages councils. Government policy is to prosecute offending employers as a last resort, which can only encourage them to take the risk and pay below the minimum. The prosecution rate is roughly one in every 1,000 offences, the fines are low in any case, so breaking the law is well worth the risk.

In the year ending June 1982, the inspectorate claimed back about £1.8 million from employers who had underpaid their workers, and were found out. But in that year, only 10 per cent of the workplaces on the register were inspected, either by a visit or letter. In 1983, about 40,000 places were checked by the inspectorate — 26,000 by visit, the rest by letter. The inspectorate has tried to compensate for cuts in its staff by placing greater reliance on postal enquiries. Ten years ago, almost all the enquiries involved a visit to the workplace. The then Labour minister for employment decided to increase the rate of inspection from one in ten establishments to one in six and, eventually, to one in four — involving, of course, an increase in the number of inspectors. The inspectorate argues that although it is still checking 10 per cent of its register each year, the work is being done more efficiently with fewer inspectors and fewer field visits. Their work is biased towards places where offences are likely to occur, including places in which workers have made a complaint to them. The inspectors claim that the 10 per cent check now is more effective than four or five years ago, and would even argue that some of the increase in the detection of illegal underpayment is due to this greater effectiveness. How far this is true is illustrated by the following example.

Juan Villegas worked as a receptionist in a licensed restaurant by the Thames embankment. For 55 hours work a week, spread over five-and-a-half days, his gross earnings were £88.

> When I started work they told me to come in at 11.15a.m. and work through till the last bill had been paid in the afternoon. This can be 3.30 or 4p.m. In the evening, I start at 7 and again I work until the last customer pays their bill. It can be 12 or 12.30 — or even as late as 2a.m.
>
> I am off Fridays and Saturday morning. It is such a small amount for the hours. They don't appreciate anything. It doesn't matter if we start in the evening a bit early. Tonight, there is a party at 6.30. I don't mind, but they don't appreciate anything you do there. I wouldn't mind if you earned well, but to get £64 in your hand takes all the interest out of it.

Juan will be 18 next birthday. Taking into account his 55-hour working week, spread over five-and-a-half days, the legal minimum weekly wage should be about £102. He was, in fact, regularly underpaid by £14 a week. The legal minimum wage for an adult in the same job would be about £128 per week. In December 1983, Juan and his co-workers were made redundant when management decided to close down for major repairs. The restaurant workers immediately contacted the wages inspectorate and an assessment is being made of the arrears that Juan is entitled to receive. Due to staff shortages, however, the inspectorate was not able to visit the place before it closed on Christmas Eve — too late to help Juan before he left the job.

Staff from the West Midlands Low Pay Unit ran a check on vacancies advertised at seven Job Centres in Birmingham, Wolverhampton and Coventry. They found that a significant number of vacancies in the wages council industries were on display at rates below the legal minimum. About 40 per cent of the adverts for jobs in hotels and catering did not state the rates of pay at all: they were simply described as 'negotiable'. One such job was at a busy pub in Birmingham centre, offering £1 an hour, cash in hand. Even assuming that the employer would correctly deduct tax and national insurance contributions before paying cash, the rate would have to be about £12.68 below the legal minimum gross wage for a 40-hour week. Although it is the responsibility of the wages inspectors to enforce the wages council rates, Job Centre staff are also government employees and are in a position to ensure that jobs on display conform to the legal minimum requirements. Yet these staff, too, have been cut, so they have little extra time for duties such as this.

Ministerial meddling

Wages inspectors and union representatives on the wages councils have argued that underpayment is made more likely by the complex nature of the orders. In the three hotel and catering wages councils, there are 42 different legal minimum pay rates, depending on the job, whether the workplace is in London or outside it, whether the worker is 16 or 17 years old, or an adult, whether the premises are licensed or not. The Licensed Residential Establishments wages council resolved in 1981 that their 31-page order should be translated into Spanish, Chinese and Urdu for the benefit of employees and employers alike. Even the employers' representative on the council stated that, if it was necessary to produce simple guidance notes in English to help people read through the order, then surely there was even more need for them to be translated into foreign languages. A letter was sent to the employment minister, seeking approval for the proposal. In 1982, the minister turned down the request: 'There are expenditure implications which need to be examined.'

The year 1983 saw unprecedented attempts by the government to intervene in the decision-making process of the supposedly independent wages councils. In August 1983, Norman Tebbit wrote to the chair of the Licensed Residential Establishments wages council, asking council members not to implement a proposed 7 per cent increase in the legal minimum rates:

> I see that the council has published proposals for changes in minimum rates which provide for increases as high as 7.3 per cent for adults and over 9 per cent for some young people.
>
> There is no doubt that the council will receive strenuous protests about changes of that order. They are likely to be harmful to businesses and jobs at a time when the real need is for the level of pay settlements to decline to sustain jobs and encourage the creation of new ones. I strongly urge the council to take serious account of representations on this point.
>
> I am sure you will let me know what the council decided when it considers representations. Confirmation of these proposals would be very damaging, and I cannot see how the council could justify such a decision to the employers and workers whose interests would be adversely affected.
>
> I am asking the Secretary to circulate this letter to all members of the council.

His letter was a challenge to the position of the independent members of the council, for clearly the union side would reject the view that a rate of £58.80 — the wage proposed for full-time service workers outside London — was excessive. Perhaps because of this meddling, the proposed increase of 7.3 per cent from October 1983 was approved without amendment, having won the support of the independent members. (However, similar intervention earlier in 1983 persuaded the Retail wages councils to revise their proposed increases downwards.) To challenge the independent members was to challenge the autonomy of the councils themselves, which was the clear intention. The appointment of independent members of wages councils is in the gift of the secretary of state for employment, by virtue of Section 2 of the 1979 Wages Council Act. No doubt the recent display of independence shown by some will have been noted by the government.

A secretary of state can also order the establishment of new wages councils in appropriate circumstances. In 1982, the TUC wrote to the Department of Employment requesting that workers in unlicensed hotels, guest-houses and hostels be brought within the wages council system. The trade unions were concerned about the depressed levels of wages in the industry, which was proving difficult to unionise (an illustration of the rates of pay in unlicensed hostels is given in chapter 5). Catering workers in licensed hotels and restaurants, cafes and snack bars are already covered by one of the Catering wages councils. Workers often move between one catering job and another, moving in and out of wages council protection depending on where they worked. The government turned down the request, as it did the ACAS proposal for a wages council for contract cleaning.

Abolition and beyond

What will happen to wages and conditions if wages councils are abolished? In 1982, Christine Craig and her co-researchers published the results of an enquiry into the abolition of six wages councils between 1969 and 1976. Together, these wages councils had set minimum rates of pay for 390,000 workers employed in industrial staff canteens, baking and confectionery, paper-box, jute, and stamped or pressed metalware industries. About 73 per cent, or 290,000, of the workers covered by these councils were women. In the wake of abolition, 'There was considerable evidence of a deterioration in pay and conditions [amongst workers] employed in the lowest grades on the lowest rates of pay.' The most striking effect of abolition was 'to increase the size of the unregulated sector of industry and therefore to raise the potential for low pay'. The researchers found no grounds to justify the decision to abolish any of these wages councils.

Jo Sinclair, a researcher at the GMBATU, was critical of the decision to terminate the Industrial Staff Canteens wages council.

> At the time it was scrapped, most workers in these canteens were directly employed. A level of about 4 per cent of staff employed by outside contractors has increased to about a third, and is still rising. Though rates of pay have kept pace with those in, for instance, the Licensed Residential Establishments wages council, other conditions have not, such as paid holidays or overtime rates. Of course, there is cost-cutting by competitive tender and much less security of employment as a result.

This view concurs with that of Christine Craig and others that staff canteen workers were 'probably in a worse position than they were before abolition'.

Will the abolition of all 27 remaining wages councils lead, as many predict, to the same collapse in pay and conditions as that which occurred ten years ago when six were scrapped? Will we witness again the same sort of erosion of workers' rights as we saw in the autumn of 1983, when the FWR was abolished? Or will abolition lead, as the government would have us believe, to the creation of more jobs?

Young workers: the substitution trick

The goverment's Young Workers Scheme (YWS) is the acid test of the Tory theory that reducing wage rates will create jobs. Sir Geoffrey Howe, when chancellor of the exchequer, gave notice of the main purpose of this scheme in a debate in the House of Commons in July 1981:

> We are working on a new scheme to offer payments to employers taking on young people under 18 at realistic rates of pay... It is the case that the machinery of wages councils has operated in some cases to price people out of jobs. In particular, these councils have done damage to the job opportunities of young people.

Under YWS, employers can claim a subsidy of £15 a week for each person they employ under the age of 18 at a wage of less than £50 a week. Employers who pay more than this lose part or all of the subsidy. Many of the wages council youth rates are above the YWS wage of £50, so that large numbers of young people are getting paid illegally low wages.

By May 1984, the scheme had covered 287,000 young employees. YWS was the result of a brainwave by the prime minister's chief economic philosopher, the monetarist Professor Alan Walters. Its purpose was to cut youth unemployment by offering young workers to employers on minimum rates in the expectation, if the theory was good, that firms would create jobs for them. Yet an investigation by the Institute of Manpower Studies, based on work carried out for the Department of Employment, showed that *94 per cent of the YWS jobs would have existed anyway.* Only six out of every 100 places on the scheme were new jobs. The results of this research have never been published by the government. The only notable achievement of YWS has been the *substitution* of adults by young workers: adult employees, paid the proper adult rate for the job, together with their annual holiday and other entitlements, have been replaced by young, heavily subsidised workers. Even adults working parttime have lost their jobs because of YWS. The failure of YWS condemns the theory that even massive wage cuts create employment.

The other main youth scheme is the Youth Training Scheme (YTS). Its aim is to provide a year's training and work experience to school-leavers starting or looking for their first job. YTS is administered by the Manpower Services Commission, and aims to provide about 460,000 places in 1984-5. Trainees can be placed in almost any workplace, where they receive a mix of work experience and off-the-job training — for example, at a college or Skill Centre. The most damaging aspects of the scheme include, again, the replacement of adults with young workers which, as the MSC itself has been forced to admit, occurs in about one in three placements. And, again, the wage rate or 'allowance' is below the comparable level set by union negotiations or the appropriate wages council. Trainees are paid a weekly allowance of £25 (£1,300 per year) by the employer, though unions can top up this figure by negotiation. In 1984, firms received a total subsidy per worker, including training allowances, of £1,950 per year.

Tom Reading worked as a YTS trainee in a London hotel. He described his experience:

> When I started, I wanted to do chefing and waiting. I was looking at different careers and thought that a chef would be a good thing for me to go into. I did some catering and home economics at school.
>
> When I started at the hotel, they showed me around and said that I had to go into the laundry there. Then, if they were short, I was a porter, almost like a dogsbody. I did this for about six months. On Thursday, we used to go to college to do social skills, run by the Training Board. A lot of people were learning nothing from the job, only from the social skills. But the Training Board can't keep an eye on the hotel manager, so the manager takes advantage. There were 21 of us when it started, but by the end it had gone right down to five. They left because they were asked to clean toilets when they were expecting to do waiting or chefing jobs. I was getting £25 a week and some travel expenses.

The comparable wages council rate for the work which Tom did was set in October 1983 at £54.80 for a 16-year-old. But because YTS people are not usually given full employee status by employers, there is considerable doubt as to whether they qualify for legal minimum wage protection. In April 1984, it was disclosed by the MSC that a quarter of teenagers who joined YTS has dropped out in the first six months. Tom's experience, if typical, suggests that frustration and boredom may well be the cause.

Breaking with convention

We have seen how, in the fields of wages councils, schemes for young workers and the FWR the government has encouraged the undercutting of wages, especially of the low-paid. Although these three policies probably make up the main thrust of the

98 / Twilight robbery

government's low-pay strategy, it manifests itself in other ways. The 1980 Employment Act abolished the right of trade unions and employers, under Schedule 11 of the 1975 Employment Protection Act, to seek compulsory arbitration in pay disputes on the fair rate for a job. Under Schedule 11, unions could submit a claim to the Central Arbitration Committee (CAC) for a legally enforceable pay award. The principle of the claims was *comparability* — either to ensure that an employer paid nationally agreed rates, or to obtain the 'going rate' for the trade in the district.

By giving trade unions the right to represent their members at the CAC, Schedule 11 helped support the development of collective bargaining; it also helped the low-paid. As Roy Lewis and Bob Simpson showed in *Striking a Balance?* nearly 2,000 claims were submitted to the CAC during its life-span, and the bulk of successful applications were on behalf of relatively low-paid workers. In different guises, legal backing has been given to minimum terms and conditions of employment for decades, as we saw with the long history of the FWR. Though these regulations have developed piecemeal, they have given at least some leverage to protect the low-paid against exploitation. Powers such as Schedule 11 were also available to employers, offering them some protection against undercutting by unscrupulous operators. Virtually the whole system of arbitration and minimum wages, built up since the end of the Victorian era, is being rapidly dismantled, for it represents, in the government's view, 'an unnecessary and unwarranted interference in employers' freedom to negotiate their own settlements'.

Pay is being undermined in other ways, too. The government is refusing to bring the Equal Pay Act fully into line with European standards, which now demand that women should be awarded equal pay with men 'for work of equal value'. A finding by the European Court that Britain's equal pay legislation was inadequate prompted government reforms — but these are considered completely insufficient by most observers, and have invited further objections in the European Court. Under Section 3 of the Equal Pay Act, women were given the right to arbitration if they believed that discrimination existed in their collective union agreement. This right has fallen into disuse because the general right to arbitration under Schedule 11 has been repealed.

Britain was one of the founder-members of the International Labour Organisation (ILO), and has put its signature to various ILO conventions governing minimum rates of pay and conditions of work. One of the main aims of the Conventions, apart from their basic humanitarian value, was to discourage wage undercutting at an international level. ILO Convention 194 requires signatory governments to include 'fair wages' clauses in public contracts. By renouncing the FWR, the Thatcher government became the first in the world to renege on an ILO Convention.

The government is unlikely to continue Britain's support for Convention 26 in 1985. This regulation requires member states to set up machinery for fixing minumum rates of pay in industries where wages are low and where collective bargaining is weakly organised. In Britain, wages councils play this part, but are now facing abolition.

The government also seems set on renouncing ILO Convention 95 which stipulates that countries should permit their citizens to be paid in current coin. In Britain, this right has been enshrined for centuries in the ancient Truck Acts. But the government is proposing reforms which break with these tradition, opening the way to payment by cheque without choice and weakening workers' rights to protest against arbitrary fines in their wage packet, as happens to shopworkers or waiting staff. A Conservative administration first gave Britain's support to Convention 95 in 1951. There is no sign that the government's wage-cutting strategy creates employment, but every indication that it creates increasing hardship for the lowest-paid.

8. Going through the motions

It is sometimes hard to believe that at almost every trade union, Labour Party or TUC conference since the election defeat of 1979, low pay has been the subject of a debate or conference motion. Hard to believe because the labour movement arrived at the threshold of the 1983 general election without a clear policy on low pay. It would have been unthinkable for Labour to have entered any election without a policy on, say, the National Health Service or council housing. Nearly one in three workers who vote are low paid. The Conservatives had installed unemployment and lower wages for those with jobs as the main devices for achieving their economic aims — cutting labour costs, raising the level of company profits, cutting public spending and inflation. It seems clear, in retrospect, that the lack of a coherent policy on low wages contributed to Labour's defeat in June 1983.

In this chapter, we identify some of the main landmarks in the low-pay debate within the labour movement between 1981 and 1984. The early 1980s have seen the development of a new economic partnership between the unions and the Labour Party, culminating in a report published in March 1983 by the TUC — Labour Party liaison committee, *Partners in Rebuilding Britain*. Yet despite conference debates and motions, TUC enquiries and other reports, low pay has failed to attain sufficient priority, reflecting the hard truth that dealing with low wages means tackling some long-standing difficulties within and between the unions.

Women: low pay, low priority

The 1981 TUC Women's Conference supported a resolution which led to the present TUC review of union policy on low pay. Three years later, this review was still incomplete. After the conference, the TUC circulated a discussion paper amongst the unions called *Low Pay and Women Workers*. It examined the reasons why women were underpaid — the segregation of women into lower-paid jobs; their concentration in the service industries; the low level of unionisation reinforced by the concentration of women in part-time work in smaller, hard-to-unionise workplaces. The report advanced a set of policies that might come within a general programme of action to help women workers.

The TUC Women's Conference of 1982 welcomed the proposals in *Low Pay and Women Workers*, many of which were included in a resolution that received unanimous support of conference. A composite motion declared that:

- the incomes policies of previous governments had failed to improve the situation of the low-paid;
- the attacks by this government on both the private and public sectors were hitting low-paid women particularly;
- the 1970 Equal Pay Act 'had failed to lift women workers out of the low-pay trap'.

The conference motion therefore called upon the TUC to include specific proposals in its economic strategy:

- the need for unions to continue to implement TUC policy on 'positive action' towards women in unions;
- special priority to be given to organising low-paid women workers;
- a campaign for a 35-hour working week, to help to reduce the 'gender gap' in earnings, due partly to men's longer working hours;
- consultation by the TUC amongst the unions about a 'statutory minimum wage for adult workers, including the pro-rata principle for part-timers'.

Pandora's Box

In September 1982, the Trades Union Congress supported a comparable resolution on low pay. In part, Congress was responding to the demands of the TUC Women's Conference, but other interests were also at work. Rodney Bickerstaffe, the new General Secretary of the National Union of Public Employees (NUPE) led a conference debate on low pay in the public services. Echoing all the frustrations of manual workers in the local authorities and health services, he declared: 'I come to the rostrum not with dry statistics, but with anger on behalf of the low-paid.' He spoke forcefully for a minimum wage level for all workers. 'What is the answer? My union believes in a statutory minimum wage. That is not embodied in the resolution; we do not want to rush things.'

Indeed, Congress would not be rushed into supporting any form of statutory minimum wage. The previous afternoon, conference had supported a resolution which 'reaffirms its support for free collective bargaining and the right of workers and their unions to negotiate their wages and conditions without interference or statutory control.' Although that motion was passed, it was disliked by wide sections of the unions present: 6,187,000 votes were cast in favour, 4,417,000 against. Why the hostility to a motion which spoke boldly in favour of the unions' time-honoured belief in free collective bargaining? The public-sector unions resented the declaration in the resolution against any form of statutory wage control: they wanted a legally enforceable minimum wage, the return of the FWR and stronger wages councils. Other unions, however, thought the motion irrelevant at a time when the TUC — Labour Party liaison committee was developing an alternative economic policy in which new forms of pay bargaining would be a major element.

Bickerstaffe, therefore, was assured of an attentive audience the following day when he asked: 'What have the arguments been against a minimum wage, or, if it comes to that, a statutory minimum wage?'

We are told that a minimum becomes a maximum.
However, a minimum becomes a maximum only if the

unions allow that to happen. We are told that a minimum would have an adverse effect on free collective bargaining. I know how my union voted yesterday, and it is clear that no union need be afraid of that. A minimum wage would provide a safety net. It would not act as an anchor to hold down the entire wages structure.

The government are trying to do away with wages councils and a 'Fair Wages' resolution. They are not removing an anchor so that all our wages can shoot up. Their purpose is to hold back the minimum because in holding that down, the rest of you are held down as well.

He also dealt with the objection that government legislation, even on minimum wages, would be a form of incomes policy:

The statutory argument is that statutory interference means an incomes policy. We have already been accused of looking two ways. My union does not regard the arguments against an incomes policy and for a minimum wage, below which no worker falls, as mutually exclusive.

He predicted that there would be more pay battles ahead — not just in the public sector, but in retailing, distribution and agriculture.

A speaker from the TUC General Council wound up the debate by observing that 'there are differences of opinion about the statutory aspect, and this is where we are trying fully to get a consensus in Congress.'

The resolution, passed without opposition, instructed the TUC to develop co-ordinated action to support the public-sector unions in the forthcoming pay round of 1982-3. It called for 'a comprehensive programme of government action on minimum wages', including four main demands:

- a strengthened wages council system;
- a restored and strengthened 'fair wages' system;
- more effective legislation on equal pay;
- consultation with affilated unions about a statutorily supported national minimum for adult workers, to be not less than £90 and linked to the cost of living.

The General Council of the TUC was asked to 'work out, prior to the election of the next Labour government, proposals on how this can be achieved'. Clearly, the low-pay debates started at the TUC Women's Conference had opened a Pandora's box of conflicting opinion.

In December 1982, the TUC circulated to all its affiliated unions a discussion document entitled *Low Pay*, which drew the unions' attention to the fact that there are low-paid workers in virtually all sectors of industry. Some 50 per cent of full-time adult women workers were low paid, defined as earning less than a minimum figure of £90 per week. The views of the unions were sought on various issues of vital concern to the low-paid: the role of wages councils and the Equal Pay Act; whether the unions preferred a statutory minimum wage or a voluntary minimum pay target without legal backing; and what part the unions' own collective bargaining could play in eliminating low pay. The document also asked whether it would be helpful for the TUC to issue guidelines for trade union negotiators. The consultation deadline was February 1983 — giving little time to develop effective discussions within the unions. So narrow were *Low Pay*'s terms of reference that many of the issues raised at recent TUC Women's Conferences on the issue were largely ignored — trade union recruitment and recognition, for instance. Nor did it reflect the ideas emerging from consultations with the Labour Party on a new economic strategy — such as the right to arbitration over claims for a fair wage and, possibly, over union recognition disputes.

Labour moves

At about the same time as the TUC was consulting the unions, the Labour Party was preparing its own report on measures to combat low pay. It would help Labour to clarify its own position for that future date when the issue would be discussed with the TUC on their joint liaison committee. Labour's discussion paper, also entitled *Low Pay*, was circulated in February 1983, well in advance of even the preliminary findings of the TUC. It called for a 'comprehensive and flexible approach' to the whole question of pay, recognising that low pay was a 'relative' idea. Pay at all levels, it stated, should be a matter for policy, although low pay — especially for women at work — was the main issue. The approach should include the restoration and improvement of such legislation as Schedule 11 and the FWR, as well as improvements to the Equal Pay Act and to the operation of the wages council system. The paper argued for a two-tier solution to low wages:

Two minimum wages	The formula	Value in February 1983
A guaranteed minimum wage for *all* workers	Half of average earnings of men in manual jobs	£80 per week £2 per hour
A voluntary minimum wage target for union negotiators	Two-thirds of average earnings of men in manual jobs	£92 per week £2.30 per hour

The lower, statutory minimum wage would be payable to all workers as of right, including those covered by wages councils. The higher, voluntary minimum wage target, on the other hand, would be arrived at by agreement between the unions and a future Labour government. The target wage, set at a level of two-thirds of average earnings of men in manual jobs, would be paid to all workers in the public sector by the end of a five-year phasing-in period — or sooner, if economic circumstances allowed. The unions would also adopt this target for their own negotiations with employers in the private sector, though it would not be legally enforced there. The lowest-paid workers in both sectors would receive the lower, guaranteed minimum wage as soon as it took effect. Recognising that workers outside the scope of union agreements were particularly low paid, the paper declared: 'the main beneficiaries of the minimum wage approach would be women workers, who form the majority of the unorganised low-paid.'

Labour's paper was first debated by a joint meeting of the

Labour Party Employment Sub-committee and the Women's Rights Study Group in February 1983. Reactions to the paper varied. Some members argued that a statutory minimum wage in some form was needed because collective bargaining by trade unions had to be ruled out as an effective way of redressing wage inequality between men and women. One reason was the under-representation of women in trade union activities. Other committee members, such as Jack Jones, argued that the committee should not underestimate the difficulties that the unions would have in reaching agreement between themselves over a voluntary pay target, let alone statutory support for a minimum wage. It was not particularly desirable to encourage the view that low wages could be abolished by a single stroke of parliament. Other issues, like the legal right for workers to be represented by unions without a complex recognition procedure, might find more ready support within the unions. But a strengthened Schedule 11 would be a more obvious priority, permitting the unions to seek arbitration on the fair rate for a job in any workplace where workers were underpaid. Jack Jones felt that the general approach to low pay had to start from the existing role of the unions, or it would end up with a state-run policy for 'one big workhouse'.

Another important argument was put forward — that the fight against low pay had to be seen in the setting of Labour's new economic strategy, which, in co-operation with the unions, was placing considerable importance on collective bargaining by unions with stronger legal back-up, such a strengthened Schedule 11. A statutory minimum wage might have the disadvantage of cutting across pay differentials and interfering with any decisions under arbitration within Schedule 11.

In turn, this view was contradicted by the opinion that though the new economic strategy had ruled out any formal pay policy between the unions and a future Labour government, there was no reason why the unions should not be able to negotiate a guaranteed minimum wage for all workers as a direct blow against low pay. There had, after all, been no objection to other kinds of statutory control on pay, such an improved Equal Pay Act or, indeed, Schedule 11 itself, which might benefit higher- as well as low-paid workers.

If there was any consensus on the committee, it appeared to be an admission that a way might be found for both collective bargaining and the statutory protection of wages to work together in an attack on low pay. Just how the two would *interact* was not altogether clear — had the paper dealt with low wages in this fashion, then the controversy which saw the two approaches as alternatives might have had a more productive result.

New partners, old priorities?

The unions and the Labour Party had devoted most of their energies to the development of a new economic strategy. In March 1983, the TUC — Labour Party liaison committee published their ideas in a report entitled *Partners in Rebuilding Britain: A Plan for Britain's Economic Recovery*. The strategy invited the unions to return once again to the centre of the stage in a new partnership with a Labour government. They would work together to bring down unemployment through planned reinvestment in industry and the public services. In the course of industrial revival, trade unions would play a key role in economic planning at national and company level. Legislation would support the development of industrial democracy, giving the unions new rights to representation and negotiation at all levels, access to company information, and equal authority with management and government. At the highest levels, the unions, through the TUC, would negotiate with the government on a National Planning Council over a wide range of economic and social issues. The process of negotiation would start with a 'national economic assessment' of prospects for industrial growth, unemployment, inflation, the balance of trade, the level of public spending. Future plans for industrial and government spending would be arrived at by a process of negotiation and would be allocated to a series of 'sector planning committees' for implementation. At the heart of the national economic assessment lies the intriguing but shadowy idea of strategy for fair wages. *Partners in Rebuilding Britain* suggests that union negotiations on pay and conditions would be supported by wage legislation, for example, on equal pay or a renewed Fair Wages Resolution.

Exactly how the strategy for fair wages would be implemented is not made at all clear, for the central theme of the report was economic recovery through industrial democracy, yet it left the impression that the stage-managers had pulled back one curtain and not the other. How were millions of low-paid, non-unionised workers to take part in the scheme? How could the proposals on fair wages benefit low-paid workers not represented by a union? Would there be new rights for union recognition in this future strategy? The TUC and the Labour Party did not meet to resolve these vital issues for the low-paid before the 1983 general election. Chapter 10 offers some speculations on how a 'fair wages' strategy might operate.

But in May 1983, the results of the TUC consultations with trade unions were published. In the report-back, various unions had expressed concern over the developing problem of low wages. The GMBATU, for example, argued that 'It is high time we started to reverse the government's success in convincing sectors of the media and the electorate that the way to solve Britain's problems is to impose low wages.' Most unions, in replying to the TUC, welcomed the idea of encouraging the reform of collective bargaining by issuing guidelines for union negotiators. They endorsed any TUC initiative to increase negotiators' awareness of low pay — especially amongst women — and to suggest tactics for eliminating it. Most unions also supported the proposal for a statutory minimum wage — though some, such as the TGWU, were strongly opposed, believing that any improvements brought about by workers' own efforts were much to be preferred to the kind of 'state paternalism' of a minimum wage. A guaranteed, minimum wage, it was argued, could discourage trade unionisation and hold wage levels down.

The TUC document was a wide-ranging assessment of trade union views. However, the unions were responding only to the questions they had been asked: the TUC had not sought views on new legislation for the right to union recognition, the recruitment and organisational difficulties of unionising low-paid workers, or how a minimum wage might operate *within* a strategy on fair wages. Most of the unions' answers were, therefore, as limited as the questions.

The 1983 general election

The sudden announcement of the June 1983 general election left the labour movement stranded without a clear policy on low pay. Labour's election manifesto proposed, in one section, 'an offensive on low pay' which seemed to face in too many directions at once. In another section, the manifesto put forward a 'better deal for women' and, elsewhere, 'equal rights at work for women'. Indeed, the manifesto is much more coherent on women's employment rights, specifically mentioning the aim of ending discrimination between the hourly rates of full-and part-time workers; the introduction of special training schemes to equip women to enter non-traditional, male-dominated jobs; the setting up of joint equal opportunity committees at work; and, amongst other proposals, the strengthening of the Equal Pay Act and a considerable increase in nursery and child-care provision, to benefit both working parents.

The Tory manifesto declared:

> National recovery has begun ... We have swept away controls on wages, prices, dividends, foreign exchange, hire purchase ... The last four years have shown that a bureaucratic machine for controlling wages and prices is quite unnecessary. It quite simply stores up trouble and breeds inefficiency.

In the shadow of the election defeat, the TUC annual conference met again, in September 1983. The government was on the point of repealing the FWR and was known to be preparing for the wholesale 'privatisation' of the health service. Congress debated low pay, aided by a TUC document. This had been circulated to the unions in August and contained the preliminary findings of the discussion document on the subject. It reached the following conclusions:

● Given the political situation in the immediate future the major issue will not be about a statutory minimum wage, but about the defence of existing statutory protection, for example, that afforded through wages councils.

110 / Twilight robbery

● The debate and discussion about a statutory minimum wage should continue.
● A major thrust of direct action to improve the position of the low-paid will need to be in the sphere of collective bargaining. There is broad support from the unions for a TUC campaign on low pay, for the reaffirmation of a commitment to a TUC low-pay target and for the TUC to issue advice and guidelines to union negotiators to help them to reach the target.

Congress supported these conclusions, adding in its low-pay resolution support for an immediate low-pay campaign which 'must strongly oppose the arguments that workers are pricing themselves out of jobs, that unemployment benefit is too high, that young workers should not be paid a living wage.'

Charged with the responsibility to implement this campaign in 1984, the TUC clearly recognises that the government is mounting an attack on wages from every conceivable angle. The government's abandonment of the FWR was seen, in TUC Economic Committee discussions early in 1984, to be 'dovetailing with its privatisation strategy', for privatisation meant a direct attack on job and income security. The direction of government policy was leading to greater inequality. The TUC therefore decided that it was vital for the unions to emphasise the issue of low pay in all aspects of their work − in public-sector pay negotiations, in TUC comments on the budget, and in negotiations with companies in the private sector. Accordingly, it was resolved to organise a conference on low pay later in the year; after that, it would publish guidelines for union negotiators. Early in 1984, the TUC updated its low-pay target to £98 per week or £2.45 an hour, being two-thirds of the average earnings of men in manual jobs.

What conclusions can be drawn from this brief account of the debate on low pay in the labour movement since 1981? First, the TUC review of low pay has progressed down a separate track from the main policy development in the 'new economic partnership'. The low-pay debate was not a tributary to the mainstream of policy. There were separate low pay consultations which really centred on the single issue of a statutory minimum wage;

elsewhere, a different 'fair wages' strategy was under consideration prior to the publication of *Partners in Rebuilding Britain*.

Second, the labour movement appears to have reached a belated recognition that low pay is the centrepiece of government policy. There was no significant campaign to oppose the abolition of the FWR; even now, there is no sign of an effective campaign in defence of wages councils. TUC initiatives to encourage the reform of collective bargaining to the advantage of the low-paid will need to be sustained for several years if they are to make any significant impact.

Finally, it is vital that the labour movement goes on to complete *Partners in Rebuilding Britain* by developing a full model for the document's half-suggested 'fair wages' strategy. To most unions, it appears that a statutory minimum wage is the only unresolved issue. Some agree on it, others do not. Yet a statutory minimum wage might be only one part of a strategy on fair wages, of no greater importance than improvements to Schedule 11, the Equal Pay Act, the FWR, rights to union recognition and other statutory wage protection — over which there is already broad agreement. Without a sudden and significant agreement on these issues, the labour movement cannot expect to be able to offer a credible alternative to the government's monetarist economic strategy.

9. Trapped in tradition? Union pay campaigns

In September 1983, the Trades Union Congress resolved that the TUC should organise a campaign against low pay. Two of the main parts of this initiative were the defence of wages councils against the government threat to abolish them, and the use of collective bargaining as a means of 'direct action by the unions to improve the position of the low-paid'. Yet on both of these strategies the trade union movement is divided. For example, long-standing objections within some unions to wages councils appear to be holding up effective campaigning. On the collective bargaining front, traditional methods have been criticised by feminists within the unions as an inadequate strategy against low pay; similar reservations about collective bargaining are held by black workers. In this chapter, we explore some of these contradictions, which must be resolved if the campaign against low wages is to make any serious headway.

Wages councils and the unions

In 1985, the government has to decide whether to renew its signature to ILO Convention 26, which requires supporting governments to maintain 'arrangements for the effective regulation of wages' in low-paid trades where collective bargaining by unions is weak, or absent. If the government renounces the Convention, it will then be at liberty to scrap the wages council system.

Trade unions are in an exceptionally strong position to take an initiative to defend wages councils and wages boards, since they are represented on almost all of them. The two exceptions are the Hairdressing and Fur wages councils. Union delegates have withdrawn from them because they have no wish to be associated with their severely low minimum wage rates. Trade unions hold a total of 309 seats on the 26 wages councils; four unions —USDAW, TGWU, GMBATU, NUTGW — have nominating rights over 87 per cent of these seats. The TGWU and the NUTGW are represented on a majority of the councils and are therefore in a key position to co-ordinate any defence campaign should they so decide (see Table 6).

Table 6 Union representation on wages councils, 1984

Union	Number of seats held	% of seats held	Number of wages councils
USDAW	85	28	9
TGWU	73	24	17
GMBATU	59	19	13
NUTGW	50	16	16
Others	42	13	20
Total	309		

Source: Department of Employment.

It would appear from the TUC survey *Low Pay* that union support for wages councils is widespread: 'Many replies imply that the wages councils have prevented very large numbers of workers from being even lower-paid,' the report concluded.

The TGWU, at its 1983 policy-making conference, fully supported composite motion 3 which called for the establishment by the TUC of a voluntary minimum wage target and which declared: 'Conference also supports the wages council system until this policy is achieved, and opposes the repeal of the 'Fair Wages' clause; and asks the TUC to campaign on these issues.'

In preparation for its June 1983 conference, the GMBATU

published *A New Strategy on Low Pay*, which declared:

> Where a concerted trade union effort is made to improve the minimum rate of a wages council, and where this is backed by some significant moves towards effective collective bargaining at a local level, progress can be made ... to raising the statutory minimum rate in that industry. Our experience of the Licensed Residential wages council over the last 10 years bears this out.

The NUTGW, also well represented on the councils, endorsed a resolution at its 1983 conference for 'a sustained campaign to oppose and resist the government's intention ultimately to abolish wages councils'. Government policy could take its members 'back to the sweatshops'.

In spite of these declared policies on the part of those unions which dominate the workers' side of wages councils, there remain serious reservations about these bodies within the unions generally. Some of the arguments which were levelled against wages councils in the 1960s and 1970s have also been levelled against the more recent demand for a statutory national minimum wage. As recently as 1981, a motion in favour of a statutory minimum wage at the TGWU policy conference was defeated. In the debate, the deputy-general secretary,

> reiterated the union's opposition to statutory controls on wages. He gave as an example the wages councils, which set minimum rates which end up as the maximum. The union's job, he argued, was to organise workers and to ensure we fight for really decent wages and conditions.

Myth or reality?

Although the TGWU has changed its policy on wages councils, such attitudes are still strongly held by many of its activists and officials. Here, we briefly consider two of the myths about wages councils: first, that 'the minimum wage becomes the maximum'.

Perhaps 15 or 20 years ago, at a time of low unemployment, the unions believed that some of the wages councils were a brake on their efforts to improve pay and conditions through collective bargaining. About 14 wages councils were abolished in that period, following union initiatives. Crucially, employers were against abolition in many cases, especially the smaller firms who, according to Christine Craig and her co-researchers, 'saw wages councils as a cheap and effective way of fixing a uniform rate, to prevent undercutting.' It was this 'uniform rate' which interfered with collective bargaining in places where unions were recognised. Employers would use wages councils as an excuse for refusing direct negotiations with unions. Without doubt, some of the same reservations about wages councils are valid today. Under conditions of mass unemployment, however, the only motive for the government wishing to abolish wages councils is to let wages drop. Employers' organisations now seem to be uniformly pro-abolition. Three million workers would be threatened by the removal of the last remaining form of wage regulation.

The second myth — that 'wages councils are a brake on unionisation' — is closely linked to the first. Employers argue that as unions already help set rates of pay on the wages councils, there is no need for them in the factory as well. But even after the abolition of wages bodies in the 1960s and 1970s, union organisation failed to flourish. Perhaps there were two main reasons. First, around the time of abolition the unions did not invest sufficient resources to pick up the organisational challenge. Many of the workers not in unions were women or immigrant workers employed in smaller workplaces, whom existing recruitment styles had failed to reach. Second, the low level of unemployment at the time helped avoid a major deterioration in working conditions; had the situation been otherwise, there might have been more recruitment. The low level of unionisation in these industries is really a question of union resources committed to organisation, rather than the responsibility of the councils themselves.

There is no shortage of arguments to defend wages councils. They are now helping to prevent a wages collapse, even though a high proportion of employers are not observing the minimum wage levels. More wages councils are needed, for the hundreds of thousands of low-paid workers who, as we saw in chapter 1, are not covered by minimum wage entitlements. Low pay encourages inefficiency amongst employers, who will recruit cheap labour rather than invest in new technology or introduce new, safer working methods. Perhaps there were days, a decade or two ago, when wages councils were used by firms to hold pay levels and union activity down. In the 1980s, they help defend the living standards of the three million low-paid workers.

Why, despite their now essential role, has the defence of the wages councils proved to be a low priority within the union movement? Overall, about a quarter of workers covered by wages councils are union members, though the proportion ranges from about 10 per cent in catering to around 40 per cent in clothing. Some 70 per cent of employees covered by the councils are women, yet about 73 per cent of the trade union delegates on them are men. Factors such as these, and the myths that surround the councils, have held back the wages councils defence initiative.

Striking a new bargain

The main aim of traditional collective bargaining methods has been to maintain differentials between skilled, semi-skilled and unskilled workers. Annual negotiations with employers are designed to protect wages against inflation and, if possible, to make real advances in working conditions. Yet many of these differentials in basic rates of pay often have far more to do with the gender or colour of the workers than the degree of skill, responsibility or risk attached to the job. For the low-paid to advance, union negotiators will have to take a hard look at the very basis of pay differentials. The intention of the TUC campaign is to achieve greater equality; traditional collective bargaining maintains the status quo. This and other contradictions of collective bargaining have to be resolved for the initiative to succeed. The TUC is organising a low-pay conference in 1984; afterwards, it will publish a set of guidelines for union representatives which are already in draft. What problems confront traditional bargaining methods, and how will the TUC's guidelines solve them?

Gender, skill and pay

'Equal pay for work of equal value' was one of the earliest demands of women trade unionists. In 1920, in her *Women in Trade Unions* Barbara Drake wrote:

> At the first Trades Union Congress of 1888, it was formally resolved for the first time that 'Where women do the same work as men they shall receive equal pay,' and mainly with this object in view, men have assisted women to organise. The principle of 'equal pay' has since then received practically unanimous support from men and women trade unionists ... in practice, however, the policy has been rarely carried out.

Traditionally, men have protected their 'right' to earn a 'family wage'. Even when jobs have become progressively deskilled, the fact that they are done by a man means they are more likely to command a higher 'skill-rating' and a higher wage than if the same work, or work of equal skill or responsibility, is done by a woman. The whole notion of 'skilled work' is shot through with gender bias. For instance, paper boxes are produced by women on hand-fed machines, requiring a lot of individual concentration. Carton-making, however, is a more automated process done mainly by men. Yet, as Jill Rubery's and Frank Wilkinson's 1979 study showed, paper-box-making was classified and paid as unskilled work, carton-making as semi-skilled. 'The women producing paper boxes are simply women producing paper boxes, they concluded, 'and however much the work itself might seem to qualify for upgrading, it remains unskilled because it is done by typically unskilled workers — women.'

Other industries offer similar examples. Elena has worked for five years in a 210-bedroom hotel in central London. As head of her department she is responsible for 27 staff: 3 assistant housekeepers; 18 room-maids; 6 linen and general porters. Her gross wage is £110 for a working week of never less than 45 hours. 'When I come in, between 7 and 7.30, I first have to prepare the lists of rooms for the maids. Then I write the job-lists for the porters — cleaning the staff and guest toilets, the common areas, the rubbish areas. By 8.30, the maids have had their breakfast so they come to collect their own lists and keys.' After that, she goes to supervise the cleaning work and the laundry. Then it is time for her to eat breakfast at her desk as she prepares the information-folders for the rooms. 'Then we — myself and my assistant housekeeper — start to go round to check the rooms. We do about 90 rooms each. In my job description, I am not supposed to check rooms, but we have been one assistant short for 18 months, so I always do.'

Her main responsiblities include line-management. She ensures that the hotel has a constant supply of clean, lettable rooms; supervises the laundry and much of the hotel's cleaning operation; controls stocks of linen, cleaning materials and equipment, baby cots, Bibles; and undertakes personnel management for 27 staff — including staff interviews, completing time-sheets, calculating weekly bonus payments.

The restaurant manager in this hotel is on the same grade as Elena, but is paid £135 per week. He is responsible for nine staff. The restaurant menu is limited to a set number of *à la carte* items. His main duties are supervision waiting staff and checking the till. There is no clear reason why the wage differential between him and Elena is £25 a week — except that each is doing what is seen as an almost exclusively 'male' or 'female' job.

Elena's position, and that of the female paper-box-makers, is fully recognised within some sections of the trade union movement. *Working Women* is one of the discussion books within the TUC's education programme, and a key resource for women's courses. The issue of low pay is given strong emphasis in the handbook:

Tackling low pay means asking some hard questions about how particular jobs are rated or valued where we work, and whether everyone has the same chance to get into higher-grade jobs ... women get stuck in the low-pay trap because traditional women's work is undervalued and because, in any organisation, women are nearly always stuck in the lower grades.

The starting-point for negotiators suggested in the handbook is to assemble the facts about the jobs men and women do, how far women are segregated into women's work and men into men's, the rates of pay and the grading system: 'Do differentials reflect skill differences — or old prejudices?' Before collective bargaining can really tackle low pay, an honest look at gender, skill and pay is unavoidable.

The annual wage claim

Union negotiators normally argue for a 'percentage increase across the board' as the basis of annual wage negotiations. But the disadvantage of this method is that it widens the gap between the highest and the lowest grades. For the low-paid to advance either means that the better-paid will have to accept a smaller percentage increase, or negotiators could use the alternative of flat-rate increases as the basis of a wage claim. In 1984, the Joint National Council, representing 900,000 local authority manual workers, negotiated a flat-rate increase of £3.40 per week. School meals staff, school cleaners, porters, gardeners and security workers would each receive the same increment. The result of the negotiations was headlined in the press as 'worth 4.5 per cent', but it was the whole wage bill which rose by this amount, not each worker's wage: the pay rise of the lowest grade was worth about 5 per cent, of the highest grade about 4.1 per cent. Union negotiators had made the point that *all* their members were low-paid, so each should receive the same cash increase. Those on the lowest grades received a small additional benefit from this approach.

At Arlington House, the hostel discussed in chapter 5, workers voted for a flat-rate wage increase in 1984. The main reason for this approach was the manual workers' desire to continue the progress made in improving their basic rates of pay following their return to work. Yet the idea was also supported by administrative and welfare staff, who accepted the principle of the manual workers' argument. There had also been a considerable increase in the number of lower-paid women workers in the hostel — in cleaning and catering jobs — who took part in the decision. It was calculated by the union negotiators that a 6 per cent increase in the total wage bill would mean an average rise per worker of £8 per week. A cubicle operatives's weekly wage would increase from £105 to £113 (7 per cent); a leading hand's would go up from £115 to £123 (6.5 per cent); and an assistant head of department would get a rise from £173 to £181 (4.5 per cent).

The cubicle staff are mainly women, who clean the residents' cubicles each day. If they had simply received a 6 per cent rise on their basic rate, it would have increased by just £6.30 a week — £1.70 less than they received under flat-rate negotiations. The union also proposed that the annual service increment of £250, payable only to white-collar workers, should be paid to all grades, including manual staff. During negotiations, management accepted both proposals in principle. Generally, the flat-rate approach has the appeal of equality between workers, and, if adopted over a series of years, will steadily improve the position of the lowest paid.

Taking seats

As the above example suggests, if low-paid workers have enough of their own representatives on union negotiating committees, then it is likely that these bodies will rearrange their priorities to tackle low pay. The TUC advocates positive action within the unions in favour of women and black workers. Two recent reports suggest that although the situation is improving, these campaigns still have a long way to go.

The first, a 1984 document produced by the Labour Research Department and entitled *Women*, reports an investigation into the working conditions of 190,000 women covered by 65 trade union agreements. In only a quarter of the workplaces surveyed did the percentage of women shop stewards match the percentage of women membership. Women were least well represented by women in agreements in the private sector. At one-third of the workplaces, branch or shop steward committees had set up equal opportunities or women's sub-committees which were discussing such issues as sexual harassment at work, equal pay, maternity leave, how to recruit more women into the union. The LRD study concluded that 'the very wide range of issues discussed suggests a developing recognition of those areas of particular concern to women workers,' and that negotiating priorities were beginning to reflect this new awareness. Such trends are a welcome move away from some of the more traditional patterns of representation. In the public sector, for example, the male school caretaker may be both the supervisor of women cleaners and their shop steward, so that the hierarchy at work is repeated in the union. Trade union branches which combine workers of different grades may be dominated by higher-paid, usually male, perhaps more articulate workers, so that the needs of women or black workers may never get discussed properly.

The second study, also published in 1984, is Colin Brown's *Black and White Britain*. He found disturbing evidence of the lack of black representatives in trade unions. Overall, about 56 per cent of Asian and West Indian employees were union members, compared with about 47 per cent of whites. Higher union membership amongst blacks was partly explained by job differences, with black workers more likly to be employed in workplaces covered by a union recognition agreement — in the public sector or in vehicle-building, for example. However, 'Despite the fact that black people are generally more likely to join a union than white people, and attend meetings with about the same frequency,' Brown found that, 'black members are much less likely than white members to hold an elected post.' In this survey, about 11 per cent of white male trade unionists said that they held some kind of position in their union, but only 4 per cent of Asians and West Indians had done so. Predictably, the proportion of women in elected posts was even lower: only 6 per cent of white women members said they were union representatives — but again, this was nearly twice as high as the proportion of black women.

Since women and black workers are more likely to be in lower-paid jobs, these findings have great significance for the TUC's collective bargaining campaign. Yet positive action can greatly strengthen union organisation. We saw in chapter 3 how Latin American workers in cleaning have developed their own section within their branch, so that the shop stewards take up members' grievances at the different workplaces and liaise with their branch as issues arise. Because shop stewards are closely in touch with their members' needs, questions on immigration are often raised at the branch — for example, on the issue of an amnesty for so-called 'illegal workers'. Workplace meetings are conducted in Spanish and English; information on negotiations or legal rights is frequently translated. Clearly, union committees need to take a hard look at the representation of low-paid workers, encouraging new delegates to step forward. The same yardstick should be applied to representation at all levels within the union movement. For instance, only 9 per cent of the 1,163 delegates to the 1982 conference of the TUC were women — even though over one-third of all trade unionists are female. Increased numbers of black and women delegates will be the best guarantee that the needs of the low-paid are taken up within collective bargaining.

Part-time work
The conditions of part-time workers are frequently neglected by union negotiators. Their hourly rates of pay and other conditions of employment are often less advantageous than those of fulltimers, a situation which mostly affects women, since around 84 per cent of all part-time staff are female. Yet part-time work is often the only option for women trying to fit together domestic responsibilities and the need to earn money.

Peggy does this double shift, looking after her family and working 20 hours a week as a bedmaker in a GLC-run hostel. All the part-time cleaners are women. In a typical week, she earns £49.64 gross, or £40 after deductions. Peggy's husband has not been able to work for four years. She told me:

> He was up painting some stonework on a church roof when he fainted. His mate caught him as he fell from the ladder. He was lucky not have been killed. His doctor first told him he had catarrh, but later they diagnosed it correctly as high blood pressure.
>
> After being on sickness benefit for a while, they put him on invalidity benefit. Then after a doctor had examined him, they said he should sign on for light work — but he's

50 now and no one would take him on, people either want a pensioner or a younger man. He was advised to take early retirement. He's paid £23 towards the rent which is £45 per week and he gets another £20-odd. We've three children at home. Unless I was earning, we couldn't pay the bills. What I earn is just paying our way. If I packed up, they'd probably pay our rent. But what else? It's a vicious circle.

The LRD enquiry into women's employment suggests that Peggy's case is fairly typical of women who work part-time. It found that part-timers were often unable to boost their earnings with bonus schemes or 'unsocial hours' payments; basic hourly rates of pay were lower and such benefits as sick pay were likely to be made only at the discretion of management. Union representatives need, therefore, to examine each of these areas to see if part-timers are at a disadvantage. They should also examine conditions in contracted-out work, because firms frequently make savings by hiving off areas like cleaning, maintenance or catering. In turn, outside contractors often make do with part-timers on wages and conditions less favourable than those of in-house staff. If contract workers are unionised already, then links need to be made with their representatives, perhaps jointly to negotiate equal terms. Once some areas of work are parcelled out without being challenged, firms will be tempted to do the same to others.

Unionisation of contract work

As firms adopt cost-saving tactics such as contracting-out, so shop stewards' committees may need to respond by encouraging the unionisation of the workers on contract. A major industrial catering company was employed to provide staff meals and refreshments at a large office block in South London. The office workers were in a print union closed shop. The father of the chapel asked one of the catering unions to try to organise the workers, who had told him that they received only two weeks' holiday a year. He found other differences in the working conditions between the contract and in-house staff:

	Office workers	Contract workers
Basic hours per week	32½	40
Minimum hourly pay	£3.35	£1.82
Annual holidays	5 weeks	2 weeks
Sick pay entitlement, first year	13 weeks	6 weeks

The catering supervisor, a woman in her mid-forties with some years of catering experience, was responsible for 24 staff — yet received £2 per week less than the lowest clerical-worker grade (i.e. what would be paid to an 18-year-old starter). Immediately the company realised that the workers were joining a union, the holiday entitlement increased to three weeks per year. The basis of the first wage claim was to establish comparability with the office workers. This would mean a substantial increase in the budget for the contract which was probably saving the print company about 50 per cent on staff wage costs. The negotiations continue.

Negotiator's checklist

The need to raise awareness of low pay amongst members and negotiators is the thread which runs through all these reservations about traditional collective bargaining. To help improve the living standards of its many low-paid members, the GMBATU published a campaigning report, *A New Strategy on Low Pay*, in 1983. The union offered detailed advice to its negotiating teams on how to improve their bargaining methods to the advantage of the low-paid. Many of the GMBATU's ideas found their way into the TUC's draft guidelines and were included in the paper on low pay discussed in chapter 8.

The TUC checklist recommends the adoption of flat-rate wage increases to help the lowest-paid. It encourages union representatives to undertake a general review of jobs within their agreement, especially those which employ mainly women. It suggests that negotiators should demand that firms open up greater opportunities for women through training and promotion schemes. Recognising the problem of poorer wages and conditions in areas of work that are contracted-out, the checklist suggests they be brought within the main negotiating structure. Various bonus payments ought to be incorporated into basic rates of pay, whilst other working conditions — such as occupational sickness and injury schemes, holidays and pensions — ought to be equally available to the low-paid.

There are some obvious omissions in the checklist. It does not, for example, emphasise the need to unionise low-paid workers within agreements or on contracts. The representation of low-paid workers on negotiating committees is not highlighted; discrimination against black workers should be specifically raised alongside that against women workers. Although they make only limited concessions to a woman's right to 'equal pay for work of equal value', recent amendments to the Equal Pay Act should nevertheless be referred to. Obviously, union negotiators will have to decide for themselves which of the many ideas in any such checklist will be most relevant to their immediate needs. One or two issues will inevitably stand out for urgent attention in the first of a number of years of negotiations giving greater priority to the specific needs of low-paid workers within union agreements.

We have suggested in this chapter that the TUC's decision to launch two initiatives against low pay — the defence of wages councils and the reform of collective bargaining — was an important first step in a counter-attack against the government's wage-cutting strategy. The contradictions within each initiative need to be drawn out if the campaign is to have serious impact. It is disturbing to reflect how our own standards on low pay are slipping. We used to say that health service workers were low paid; now their conditions are being defended against cuts being introduced by private contractors. Opposition to privatisation is clearly the vital third element needed to complement the TUC initiatives on wages councils and collective bargaining.

10. Strategy for a fair wage

There is no package solution to the low-wages problem. The recent debate on low pay in the labour movement shows only too clearly that some basic questions still have to be settled — on the role of the unions and a future Labour government in tackling low wages, on policies to deal with unequal pay for women and black workers, on the relationship between legislation against low pay and free collective bargaining.

Since the 1979 election defeat, the Labour Party and the TUC have been searching for a new unity and an economic programme based on partnership rather than conflict. Labour's election defeat followed the traumatic 'winter of discontent' of 1978-9, when low-paid workers in the public services struck against the government's refusal to award them pay rises above its incomes policy target of 5 per cent.

The new economic strategy which has emerged out of these ruins represents a break with previous Labour Party programmes from 1973 onwards when economic policies, loosely termed for the first time the alternative economic strategy, were based primarily on the extension of state control. These alternative strategies have taken different forms since the early 1970s, but their main elements have included, first, an increase in public spending to prevent unemployment and raise living standards and, second, an industrial strategy based on public ownership and planned investment.

The labour movement's most recent alternative strategy is set out in *Partners in Rebuilding Britain*, which is primarily a plan for the recovery of full employment in the British economy. As was discussed in chapter 8, it places the trade unions once again at the centre of national affairs in partnership with a new Labour government. Under this new strategy, unions, government ministers and employers would meet on a National Planning Council. The framework for talks would be a 'national economic assessment', which would be concerned with two main priorities. The first would be the creation of jobs for the unemployed through government-led investment plans. The second call on resources would be to improve the 'living standards for those most in need, including pensioners, recipients of state benefits and the low-paid'. The process of reaching agreement in detail would reflect at national level the methods and objectives of collective bargaining. This is the essence of the new partnership. The report also suggests that, in each industry and service, a 'sector planning committee' would be established with representatives from unions, employers and government. These committees would co-ordinate and plan investment, allocating funds to particular companies in consultation with their union representatives. Industrial democracy would develop in such companies through new rights to workers' representation, assisting them to take an active part in investment decisions, including the number and type of new jobs that would be created. New rights to company information would ensure that representatives were adequately equipped for the task. As *Partners in Rebuilding Britain* states, 'The key to the national economic assessment is that collective bargaining at plant and company level would take place in a wider context.'

The third course

Within the idea of a national economic assessment lies the further suggestion of a 'fair wages' strategy, which would tackle low pay, encourage the establishment of fair wages for a job and fair differentials between jobs. How would the National Planning Council members operate such a strategy? Clearly, it would not be a government-led incomes policy, for the unions would not accept government control on pay, even if the reward was a dramatic reduction in unemployment. Nor would the government accept a collective bargaining free-for-all. The 'fair wages' strategy would have to find, through the process of bargaining, a third course to help develop a fair incomes structure. Fair wages would be achieved through collective bargaining at company level by the unions, but their negotiations would be supplemented by new legislation on pay. *Partners in Rebuilding Britain* mentions only briefly the kind of legislation that would be required:

> Union strategies to eliminate low pay will be supported by agreement on the social wage and by the restoration and improvement of legislation such as Schedule 11, the 'Fair Wages' resolution, wages councils and the Equal Pay Act. Arrangements to ensure fair wage relativities will be greatly supported, both by the establishment of agreed mechanisms, to which negotiators in the public services could have recourse where this is required, and by the pursuit of complementary policies on taxes, benefits and the distribution of income and wealth.

All jammed into one paragraph. What is an 'agreed mechanism'? Obviously something which was not agreed at the time of writing or it would have been spelt out. Yet the main ideas for legislation are familiar. One of the attractions of the strategy is that it sees collective bargaining and legislation on pay as supporting each other. Significantly, proposals for a *statutory* minimum wage are not included because discussion was still taking place within the unions on this issue when the report was published.

Involving the bystanders

Partners in Rebuilding Britain shows how far the centre of gravity of Labour's industrial policy has shifted in favour of creating a role for working people. Roy Green, writing in the *New Statesman* in September 1983, saw the shift as 'reflecting the interests and demands of union members at shopfloor level ... reducing the ability of employers to control the agenda for collective bargaining, giving workers direct leverage over crucial investment decisions'. The report remains an important step forward in the evolution of any coherent alternative plans. Yet, as we have seen, it was published whilst separate consultations were still proceeding within the Labour Party and the TUC on how to tackle low pay. Therefore, its ideas on the problem of extending basic union recognition rights to millions of low-paid, under-unionised workers are not surprising: they seem to be bystanders who may look upon the spectacle of the new economic strategy, but can they play an active part?

Anne Phillips, in her book *Hidden Hands: Women and Economic Policies*, criticised existing alternative economic strategies on two counts: first, that they want simply to create more of the same kinds of jobs, rather than trying to establish equality of working and living conditions between men and women; and, second, that traditional collective bargaining methods have failed to eliminate low pay, particularly amongst women and black trade unionists. If collective bargaining is to be the starting-point for the 'fair wages' strategy' then, as we have suggested in chapter 9, union negotiators will have to take far greater account of the needs of the low-paid.

The strategy clearly requires new procedures to assist non-unionised workers to obtain union recognition, such as those suggested in chapter 6 and on page 130. Furthermore, negotiations between unions and employers will be able to go only so far in creating a fair system of wages for jobs and fair relativities in pay between different jobs. Collective bargaining would have to be supplemented by new legislation — on the right to arbitration over wage disputes, on equal pay and perhaps on a statutory national minimum wage. Workers' access to many of these rights would be through their trade union so that new legislation would be able to play a part in supporting union activities. We can speculate further on how the 'fair wages' strategy might be put together. (Figure 1: A 'fair wages' strategy.)

Support for collective bargaining

Overall responsibility for co-ordinating the strategy to support collective bargaining would be given to a **Fair Wages Board**. Its membership might include representatives from the unions, employers' organisations and independent members. Its brief would be to ensure the implementation of the strategy, and its two main areas of responsibility would be to co-ordinate the work of the Industrial Arbitration Boards and to oversee the operation of new legislation. In itself, the board would have no arbitration role, but it would be expected to ensure consistency between the decisions taken by the different bodies for which it is responsible.

Industrial Arbitration Boards would be established for each industry and public service, with membership drawn from the same three areas as the main Fair Wages Board. The Arbitration Boards would act as the 'front line' of the main Fair Wages Board and would be responsible for resolving disputes on two main issues: union recognition and wage claims. Where workers have been frustrated in their efforts to obtain union recognition, their trade union would have the right, under new legislation such as that referred to in chapter 6, to submit a claim to arbitration. Whilst an Arbitration Board was deliberating on the recognition claim, it might also resolve any dispute over wages and conditions. Boards would therefore require powers, similar to those in Schedule 11 of the 1975 Employment Protection Act, to arbitrate over pay disputes. In reaching their decisions the boards would be expected to ensure that a 'fair wage' was set for jobs involving a similar degree of skill, responsibility, training, risk, etc., and that fair differentials were established between different grades of jobs. The boards would be expected to encourage the spread of the leading rates negotiated by unions for any particular job in their industry. At the same time, they would have to ensure consistency between decisions on pay for the same job in different sectors — for example, cleaners in the NHS and on private contract. To assist them in this task, the Fair Wages Board would offer detailed guidance and information on settlements being reached by the different boards. In this way, a common rule for jobs involving similar skills would be established. Clearly, there is no reason why the boards should not also adjudicate over claims from women or black trade unionists for 'equal pay for work of equal value'.

Wages councils would be reconstituted into mini-Arbitration Boards for industries where wages and conditions are acknowledged to be particularly low. Their membership would again be the same as the main Fair Wages Board, so that the 'independent' members of the old wages councils would no longer be voting for one side or the other, but would be arbitrating with other board members on evidence presented by unions and employers for the annual revision of wages and conditions. The mini-boards might also be expected to establish fair rates for jobs in their sector, as compared with the bare minimum rates set by today's wages councils. The wages inspectorate would enforce these rates, being directly accountable to the mini-board. Trade unions would be able to refer complaints of underpayment direct to the inspectorate, whereas at present only individual workers can do so.

Public-sector workers — in the civil service, local government, the health service, and so on — might be covered by a **Public-Sector Pay Commission**. The commission's members would be drawn from the same three areas as the main board, and would be responsible for reassessing pay and working conditions for all grades within the services. During this assessment, unions and employers' organisations would submit their evidence. The commissioners' recommendations would be submitted to the appropriate joint negotiating body for each service and to the Fair Wages Board. Unions would have the right to refer to any disputes over wages and conditions which might arise against the background of this reassessment of public-sector pay to the Arbitration Board for their particular service.

Over time, these bodies would supplement collective bargaining by the unions, helping to develop in their decisions a pattern of fair wages for similar jobs. Though the boards would accept union claims on behalf of workers of all grades, the low-paid would have the most to gain from the general brief of the boards to ensure fair wages, eliminate unequal pay and facilitate union recognition.

132 / Twilight robbery

Figure 1 A 'fair wages' strategy

Collective Bargaining

by Trade Unions *supported by*

New rights to arbitration

New legislation

Arbitration

Industrial Arbitration Boards

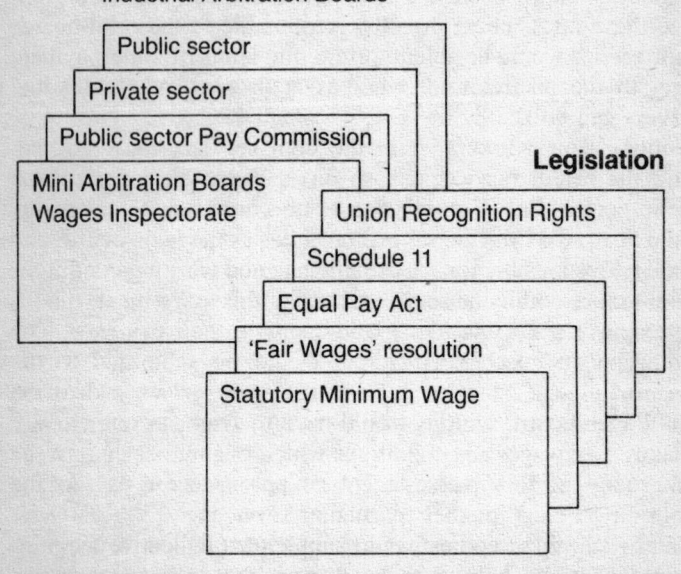

- Public sector
- Private sector
- Public sector Pay Commission
- Mini Arbitration Boards
- Wages Inspectorate

Legislation

- Union Recognition Rights
- Schedule 11
- Equal Pay Act
- 'Fair Wages' resolution
- Statutory Minimum Wage

Fair Wages Board

Membership

Union representatives

Employers representatives

Independent members

Responsibilities

To ensure the implementation of the 'Fair Wages' strategy

To coordinate the work of the Arbitration Boards

To oversee the new legislation

'Fair wages' legislation

How might the new legislation in these areas operate? Chapter 7 showed the role of the 'Fair Wages' resolution and Schedule 11 in giving trade unions the right to ensure that firms paid recognised minimum rates negotiated on a national or industry basis, or, failing that, the local 'going rate' for a trade or industry. The main shortcoming of Schedule 11 was that it had no jurisdiction over the claims above national minimum rates, so it did not help the spread of 'leading' trade union rates for a job. Also, comparisons could only be made between workers doing the same job.

A way forward lies in the lifting of these restrictions on arbitration, so that the three principles of the 'fair wages' strategy might include: a fair wage for each job; comparability between jobs of a similar skill, responsibility, risk or training requirement; and setting fair differentials between jobs of a genuinely different grade. A new Schedule 11 would operate on a more general basis than a new Equal Pay Act which, though necessary, would eliminate only those differences in pay which discriminate solely on the grounds of the gender of the worker.

What are the main limitations of the existing Equal Pay Act? First, to claim equal pay, a woman has to find a man doing like work in her firm to compare herself with — a difficult problem given that so much of womens' low-paid work is done by women alone. The second hurdle has been the need to convince a tribunal that she was indeed doing 'like work'. In 1982, just six of the equal pay cases heard by tribunals were successful. As we saw in chapter 7, the government has responded to criticisms of the British legislation in the European Court by amending it so that women doing a different job from a man may claim 'equal pay for work of equal value'. Yet the Conservatives' new legislation still applies only to workers in the same firm, and employers will be able to claim that 'market forces' justify paying women less. New equal pay rights should remove these restrictions on 'equal value' claims, allowing a much broader basis for comparability between men's and women's earnings. With the return of the right to arbitration, discrimination in collective union agreements would once again come under scrutiny.

The statutory minimum wage debate

A legally enforceable national minimum wage could be one of the pieces of legislation underpinning collective bargaining. The idea is, however, a controversial one. Some trade unionists believe that it would undermine rather than underpin their activities. Those who support the statutory minimum wage (SMW) argue that it would guarantee that no worker would receive less than the target minimum wage set by the National Planning Council; the level of the SMW is most likely to be the TUC's minimum wage target, that no worker should receive less than two-thirds the average earnings of men in manual jobs. As we have seen, early in 1984 this would have been about £98 per week, or £2.45 an hour for part-timers. The SMW would benefit all low-paid workers, especially women, migrant and immigrant workers and would therefore be an *equal* minimum wage for all those in low-paid occupations. It would ensure immediate improvements in the living standards of the low-paid in the first year of operation of the 'fair wages' strategy. Its supporters see the SMW in the same light as a new Equal Pay Act — as only one of a number of legal rights in a strategy to supplement collective bargaining, and so improve the wages of millions of the lowest-paid who are not yet represented by unions or who are stuck at the bottom of the wage scales in an agreement.

Some trade unionists object to the SMW on principle, arguing that it contradicts the idea of free collective bargaining; it would, they fear, become a kind of back-door incomes policy which would lead to controls on wages at all levels. Once set, the annual increase in the level of the SMW would be used as a pay 'norm' by a future Labour government to control the level of *all* wage increases, not just those of the lowest-paid. Further objections to the SMW echo those levelled against minimum rates set by wages councils. For instance, it is feared that the SMW would discourage the low-paid from ever joining a union. Why should they bother when the state can provide a minimum wage? The critics believe that the minimum wage would become the maximum in many workplaces. Employers would refuse to offer pay rises to any staff paid above the minimum on the grounds that they could not afford to, and the better-paid would object. Thus, it is claimed, the SMW could soon backfire on the unions. In general terms the SMW would cut right across collective bargaining, sweeping away some carefully constructed pay differentials at the lower end of wage scales in union agreements. It is, so the argument goes, different in principle from the Equal Pay Act, which discriminates against unfair differences in pay based solely on the gender of the worker. On this basis, the Equal Pay Act is compatible with collective bargaining, but the SMW is not.

In response, supporters of the SMW reply that it would discriminate against *all* forms of low pay, not just low pay for women. It would, for example, encompass low pay amongst migrant workers, who have no direct legislative protection. If a future Labour government were to pervert the use of the SMW into a kind of incomes policy, this would indeed be a breach of faith. The level of the SMW should be arrived at by negotiation between the unions and the government, not imposed by one side upon the other. Furthermore, the 'fair wages' strategy allows for arbitration on wages claims, so the minimum wage is unlikely to become the maximum. In any case, argue SMW advocates, it would only squeeze those differentials between jobs at the bottom end of the wage scale. Fine differences in pay at these low levels have more to do with the gender, colour or bargaining power of workers than with any fair assessment of the true rate for the job. Many of the lowest-paid in the private sector are on wage council rates, or are not covered either by a union agreement or a wages council. In these cases, union agreements would not be radically disturbed.

The claim that the SMW would undermine the development of trade unionism in the private sector is rejected on the grounds that the 'fair wages' strategy also includes rights to assist workers to obtain union recognition and a fair wage. Once collective bargaining rights had been established, the low-paid could expect to obtain further improvements in pay and working conditions well above the SMW. In the public sector, as we saw in chapter 8, the trade unions support the SMW.

If the advocates of the SMW have a practical argument in their favour, it is to be found in the answer to the legitimate question: would the unions be able to cope with the probable flood of union recognition and wage arbitration claims on behalf of the low-paid that would follow the new rights to arbitration? The main flow is likely to stem from thousands of small and medium-size workplaces in the service industries. To meet this immediate problem, the SMW should perhaps be established in the first phase of the 'fair wages' strategy to bring a general immediate benefit to the low-paid and to stifle wage undercutting against those who sought arbitration over a fair wage. It might be possible to phase out the SMW entirely over a few years; even if it did remain, it would become less and less relevant to the bulk of workers. Undoubtedly, some union hostility to the idea of a statutory minimum wage has been encouraged accidentally by the way the TUC conducted its low-pay consultations with the unions. The 'debate and discussion' on the SMW took place as if this were a policy on its own, as if it were *the* solution to poverty wages. Seen in isolation, it is of course a type of incomes policy for the seven million low-paid. In its proper setting — within the strategy for a fair wage — it would be only one positive element in a programme to eliminate working poverty.

End low pay!

As we have seen, there is no simple solution to low pay. It exists in all industries and services, inside and outside the sphere of influence of the trade unions. To tackle low pay, a many-sided approach is evidently needed. It should be based upon workers' own influence, supported by new legislation and the general right to arbitration over disputes. The crisis of low pay represents a major challenge to the labour movement. Can it unite around a strategy capable of creating fair wages and greater equality out of exploitation?

The government's wage-cutting strategy is returning industrial conditions in Britain to the Victorian era. The various kinds of wage and job protection which have existed in one form or another for the best part of this century have almost all been abolished or deliberately weakened. When, in 1979, the government first announced its decision to abolish the arbitration powers of Schedule 11, the Engineering Employers Federation and other employers' organisations publicly deplored the move, fearing that rogue firms would undercut their national agreements. Now, in 1984, employers' representatives on wages councils are generally pro-abolition. They have swung round to give full support to the government's wage-cutting plans. Yet there are at least two important differences between the position of low-paid workers now and at the end of the Victorian period: the trade unions and the modern welfare state.

To the government and its monetarist advisers, the mere existence of trade unions is an unacceptable interference in their vision of a free market for labour. In low-paid industries, anti-union practices by employers are encouraged by a government which, early on, abolished measures to help the development of collective bargaining amongst unorganised workers. At the same time, supplementary and unemployment benefits at present offer people out of work some protection from having to take 'a job at any price'. But monetarists argue that however low wages may fall, the level of benefits should fall that much lower. They are saying this because destroying wage controls has not had the desired effect of 'pricing people back into work'. Indeed, in 1984 the government initiated a review of the social security system. Though there are many inequalities in the system which call for reform, there is widespread suspicion that the review is a cover for substantial reductions in benefits.

Low pay is becoming more important with every day that goes by, with every decision by the government or employers to undermine unions and jobs. Working out strategies to tackle unemployment is familiar ground for the labour movement. But fresh solutions are now needed for familiar problems that have come to occupy an unfamiliar place — at the *centre* of economic affairs. It is time to act on low pay, inequality and frustrated union organisation. How we respond may determine whether we can halt the government's rough ride back to Victorian Britain.

A guide to reading

Chapter 1

Useful facts and figures on the extent of low pay in Britain are given in a series of publications by the Low Pay Unit, including *Low Wages and Poverty in the 80s* (Low Pay Unit, 9 Poland St., London W1: 1983). Chris Pond discusses the importance of wages councils to the low-paid in 'Wages councils, the unorganised and the low-paid', in chapter 8 of G.S.Bain (ed.), *Industrial Relations in Britain* (Basil Blackwell, Oxford: 1983). Paul Harrison's *Inside the Inner City* (Penguin, Harmondsworth: 1983) suggests that government economic policies, are creating similar conditions of 'underdevelopment' as exist already in Third World countries. The estimates of future employment growth in Britain are taken from a publication by the Hotel and Catering Industry Training Board's *Meeting Future Needs* (PO Box 18, Wembley, Middlesex: 1983). Jenny Beale's *Getting it Together: Women as Trade Unionists* (Pluto Press, London: 1982) includes an analysis of low pay amongst women and suggests ways forward in the unions. Colin Brown's *Black and White Britain* (Policy Studies Institute, 1 Castle Lane, London SW1: 1984) provides an assessment of discrimination in employment, including trade union activities and earnings.

Chapters 2 – 5

A well-researched history of trade union organisation in the hotel industry is given in Paul Soto and Liz Dronfield's *Hardship*

Hotel (Counter Information Services, 9 Poland St., London W1: 1980). *El Mopo (The Mop)* is the newsletter of cleaning workers in London, and is available from Latin American Workers Association, Beauchamp Lodge, 2 Warwick Crescent, London W2. *Community Action Magazine* no.63 contains an appraisal of the unionisation of Arlington House hostel (available from 29 Clerkenwell Close, London EC1). *SHOPtalk* is a magazine encouraging shopworkers to unionise, published by a shopworkers' co-operative (available from 13, Ingestre Place, London W1). Two reports by the Migrants Action Group describe the campaign by community and trade union organisations to fight the deportation of migrant workers, many of whom were employed in the catering trade: *Migrant Women under Threat* and *On the Road to Repatriation* (available from Migrants Action Group, 68 Chalton Street, London NW1: 1980 and 1981). Simon Crine and Clive Playford wrote *From Rags to Rags* (Low Pay Unit, London: 1982). The issue of national insurance contributions and the low-paid is examined in the *Low Pay Unit Review* (June 1984).

Chapter 6

Striking a Balance? by Roy Lewis and Bob Simpson (Martin Robertson, Oxford: 1981) details the employment legislation repealed by the government when it first came to power. John McIlroy's *Trade Union Recognition and the Limits of the Law* (Workers Education Association, London: 1979) is a critical review of Labour's legislation intended to assist unorganised workers to obtain union recognition. The *1982 Annual Report of the Advisory, Conciliation and Arbitration Service* includes a summary of the process of conciliation around the Tuttons restaurant strike.

Chapter 7

The history of the 'Fair Wages' resolution is discussed in *Back to the Sweatshops* (Low Pay Unit, London: 1982). The Conservative Party's 1983 election manifesto is essential (though not bedtime) reading for an understanding of the wage-cutting strategy. A vital study of the disastrous consequences of abolition of wages councils is found in Christine Craig and others, *Labour Market Structure, Industrial Organisation and Low Pay* (Cambridge University Press: 1982). They studied the results when six wages councils were scrapped in the 1970s. Chris Pond's article in the *New Statesman*, 'Generation Gap'(6 January 1984) destroys the myth that the Young Workers Scheme is pricing young people back into jobs.

Chapter 8

The TUC discussion paper *Low Pay and Women Workers* (1981) contains important proposals for a campaign against low pay among women. The report of the 1982 Trades Union Congress includes the debate on low pay and the statutory minimum wage. The report submitted to the 53rd Womens' TUC and the report of the conference both contain information on policy and resolutions reflecting widespread concern amongst women trade unionists on low pay. Available from TUC, Congress House, Great Russell Street, London WC1.

Chapter 9

Working Women, by the TUC Education Department (1981) is a stimulating pamphlet, useful for union negotiators concerned about unequal pay among women members. The Labour Research Department's report, *Women* (January 1980), includes useful facts on the working conditions of women covered by union agreements. Two articles in *Feminist Review*, Issue No. 10, assess the position of women at work: Angela Weir and Mary McIntosh, in 'Towards a wages strategy for women', look at the failures of traditional collective bargaining by unions to deal with low pay and suggests a range of new policies for the unions; Anne Phillips and Barbara Taylor, 'Sex and skill' (issue no.6) examines the argument that waged work is sharply divided along sexual lines. *A New Strategy on Low Pay* was published by the General, Municipal and Boilermakers Union for their 1983 conference and recommends various improvements to collective bargaining to assist the low-paid. The TUC's *Workbook on Racism* was issued in 1983; it includes some interesting examples of unionisation struggles by low-paid black workers.

Chapter 10

Partners in Rebuilding Britain was issued by the TUC—Labour Party liaison committee in March 1983 (available from the Labour Party). It outlines the new economic partnership within the labour movement's 'alternative economic strategy'. Anne Phillips, in her book *Hidden Hands: Women and Economic Policies* (Pluto Press, London: 1983) brings together a range of criticisms of the strategy, with its overwhelmingly male bias. Roy Green reflected on the strategy after the 1983 election defeat in 'Going forward', in the *New Statesman* (23 September 1983). *The Case for a National Minimum Wage* was written by Chris Pond and Steve Winyard for the Low Pay Unit in 1982.

It is also worth reading Jo Morris, *No More Peanuts* (National Council for Civil Liberties, London: 1984) which suggests ways to use the new rights for women to claim 'equal pay for work of equal value'. Patricia Hewitt and Bill Birtles, *Your Rights at Work* (National Council for Civil Liberties, London: 1983) is a useful handbook on wage and employment protection. *Making the Wages Councils Work for You* is the title of two booklets issued by the Low Pay Unit (1983), which give brief and simple explanations of legal minimum entitlements.

List of abbreviations

AAG	Arlington Action Group
ACAS	Advisory, Conciliation and Arbitration Service
CAC	Central Arbitration Committee
CCMA	Contract Cleaning and Maintenance Association
CHAR	Campaign for Homeless and Rootless
DHSS	Department of Health and Social Security
EPCA	Employment Protection Consolidation Act 1978
FECODE	Federacion de Educadores de Colombia
FWR	Fair Wage Resolution
FWS	Fair Wages Strategy
GMBATU	General, Municipal, Boilermakers and Allied Trades Union
ILO	International Labour Organisation
NUTGW	National Union of Tailors and Garment Workers
SMW	Statutory Minimum Wage
TGWU	Transport and General Workers Union
TUC	Trades Union Congress
USDAW	Union of Shop, Distributive and Allied Workers
YTS	Youth Training Scheme
YWS	Young Workers Scheme